WRITING THE SH

Writing the Short Story

By
ROY LOMAX

LONDON

Roy Lomax
WRITING THE SHORT STORY
© Copyright, Roy Lomax 1983

First Published 1983

ISBN 0 906486 13 0

Writing School Guides
Published in Great Britain by
CLAREFEN LIMITED
18–20 High Road, Wood Green
London N22 6BX

Set by Santype International Ltd., Salisbury
and printed and bound by Billing & Sons Limited Worcester.

Contents

Chapter One

WHAT IS A SHORT STORY

'Not that the story need be long, but it will take a long while to make it short.' THOREAU

We can certainly trace the origins of the short story back to 6,800 years ago when the greatest of all pyramid builders, King Cheops, ruled Egypt. We can date it back that far with a great degree of accuracy. It was apparently the custom of Lord Cheops to gather his sons around his throne and have them tell tales of the magicians of ages gone before. How old these tales were when Cheops sat listening enthralled is anyone's guess. So there is no doubt that the short story as an art predates the work of Homer or any known poet. And you will be immensely satisfied to learn that the evidence so far discovered gives us short stories long before the boring clay tablets of the tax-gatherers and the conclusions of government officials. Those ancient Egyptians certainly had their priorities right!

To get the whole situation straight, we must also add that King Cheops was of a family that was dedicated to taking over the priest-hood of the sun-god and appointing themselves popes, if not aspir-ing to godhood itself. For the short story was the principal weapon of the priest, the magician, and the sage. It has also been the un-deniably effective art of all the important religious and political reformers since before the days of Buddha. Shakespeare based all of his plays on tried and tested short stories. Even now there are primitive races whose behaviour is determined by the tribal mysteries told in short story form by the elders or the ju-ju man. If the hunter is failing at catching meat for his hungry belly, he will pay for pro-fessional help, which will sometimes be in the form of a talisman, a concoction or a spell – but will *always* be accompanied by a short story.

For, to the hunter, these tales are of immense practical importance. They are full of mystic secrets which teach him that there can be more to his life than an acceptance of what fate serves to him. He also hears tales around the camp fire which teach him the sense of wonder, of humour and affection and of honour. We may laugh at these stories of talking plants, animals and pieces of rock, yet we tell our own young children almost identical tales in order to educate and amuse.

There is true magic in the telling of a good short story. It is not very fashionable these days to speak in such terms as this. How can there possibly be any magic in a story, we may be asked. Well, nobody is claiming that there can be magic in a short story. What we said was, in the *telling* of a short story. And there lays a great world of difference. It isn't so much what you say, as how you say it.

Have you ever suffered from the dismal and embarrassing experience of listening to a joke told by a person who hasn't the slightest idea of how it should be done? Have you been told the 'punch-line' first, so that the whole impact of the story has been lost? Or been told, between uncontrollable guffaws, that this really is something funny that you are being told? You surely have. Awful, isn't it? The 'magic' of the short story – and the joke – is what is invested by the teller. It is the carefully planned intention to catch your attention, and then to take you by the hand and lead you to experience a world which exists only in imagination. It is a technique which is as old as story-telling itself. And it will remain effective for as long as there is a human being to hear or read a story, for the technique is based on satisfying a basic appetite within the human character. Find a person who has absolutely no interest in a well-told story, and you will discover somebody who is hardly human at all.

Of course, people will have their individual tastes. We must not expect the hairy-armed man of action to pick up the average women's magazine with delighted anticipation. Nor the middle-class mum to pick up a western with her weekly shopping. But people do have their individual tastes, and surprises should not be so surprising. We can cover this rather briefly by saying that any particular well-told story will be most acceptable to people who like that sort of thing.

Story-telling never has and never will lose its popularity. Styles of writing may change, and so may subjects. But the characters in stories will virtually remain the same, as will their passions, their viewpoints, their responses and their basic human goals.

We have already mentioned King Cheops. He was succeeded by a fellow Egyptian by the name of Khafri somewhere about 4,800 B.C. There is a short story which is attributable to him:—

King Nebka was sore from his long journey. He called his chief steward unto him and said, 'We are near to the house of Ubauaner, my old friend and teacher. We shall visit him in order that I may be refreshed and enjoy his company once more.'

They arrived at the house of Ubauaner and he welcomed King Nebka with kisses and loyal salutations. The wife of Ubauaner kneeled before the king and kissed his feet. As she rose, her eyes met those of one of the king's servants and her heart was immediately pierced with the arrow of love. Returning quickly to her chambers, she sent her maid to the man with costly gifts, and had her maid say, 'There is a house by the lake, where I go to rest each afternoon. It would please me if you come and let us enjoy our company together.'

The manservant did as he was bade and enjoyed the many refreshments and other gifts which were pressed upon him.

Seeing her mistress so disposed, the maid said to herself, 'My mistress is most incautious with this man and will most certainly be discovered. Then shall I be accused of conspiring against the honour of our master, Ubauaner, and I shall be burned and fed to the crocodiles.'

With much wailing and distress she went unto the chamber of Ubauaner, kneeled before him, and acquainted him with the behaviour of her mistress with the servant of the king.

And so the story continues to the unhappy end of the foolish couple. Allowing for what must certainly have been lost during translations and retranslations, the story is as fresh today as it was nearly 7,000 years ago. As the French say: 'The more things change – the more they remain the same.'

Buddha, who was born about 600 B.C. also told stories that have stood the test of time for their wit and humour. The surprising tale of The Monkey and the Queen's Jewels and the interesting Tale of Princess Sambula are generally considered to be masterpieces of short fiction. Most of Buddha's works were written up in the 14th century by a Greek called Planudes and wrongly attributed to

Aesop. The Ass in the Lion's Skin, which appears in Aesop's Fables certainly originated from Buddha, and the earlier version is superior to the later one.

Buddha said that his stories were based on the experiences of his previous 550 lives in the forms of various animal and human bodies. You are free to believe that or not as you choose, but there is a great *reality* about them as fiction. One final word on Buddha is to mention his interesting The Judgment of Buddha. An almost identical version of this appears in the Old Testament as The Judgment of Solomon. There has obviously been a great deal of story-telling over the past 7,000 years – including who wrote what!

Dictionaries can give many definitions of the word story. For our purposes here, the most suitable would be 'an account of an incident'. And by incident, we mean 'a distinct piece of action'. We can get fairly close to accuracy for the purposes of the author to say that a story is an account of a factual or fictional piece of action, or several pieces of action, which relate in some way to give a seemingly overall action on a larger scale. Standing to one side from the subject of the short story for a moment, it will be seen that this is where the writer of a book-length story can fail, by attempting to knit together a number of pieces of action which relate poorly to each other and do not gel into one large piece of action. The writer in this case, probably without realising it, has written a number of short stories with different actions.

In any story, be it short or long, there should be an apparent road or backbone running through the whole piece. In a strange kind of way, the reader should feel that he has travelled a smooth and easy journey, even if his attention has been fixed on blood or mayhem along the way.

So much for our definition of the word story. Now what do we mean when we say a short story? How short is short? How long is long? How long is a piece of string? This is not the way to approach the answering of this question. Just remember what we said before, 'a story is an account of an incident'. If the incident can be quickly told then, obviously, the story is going to be quick in the telling – a very short story. The size of the room decides the amount of carpet required to cover it. This is a very accurate way of defining how long a story should be, but if we hope to sell our stories, then another and quite different factor comes into the game. And that is 'preferred length'. What does the editor require as a minimum and maximum number of words? What *exact* length of time does it have to fill if read on radio?

If the majority of markets available to you have their own individual preferred story length requirements, and if the incident of a story determines to a large extent just how long that story should be, then you will realise that your stories *must* be selected and tailored carefully before the writing is even begun. The best advice that can be given to the budding writer is — always decide the approximate length of a piece before you begin to write it.

We can, simply by rule of thumb, give descriptions to story lengths. We can say that a short-short story would be somewhere between 1,750 and 2,500 words. The short story could consist of up to 15,000 words. A story that was about as long as this book could be called a novella, or a mini-novel. Up to 120,000 words would be the length of a novel. And above that there are the books which are commonly referred to these days as block-busters.

The short-short story begins at 1,750 words. A story shorter than that is more properly called a vignette. You will just occasionally come across a vignette in a modern publication, but they are not generally favoured and generally read with a feeling of lack of substance. It usually takes all of 1,750 words in which to relate a single significant incident, at the same time introducing some colouring and characterisation. Unless you decide to specialise in the short-short and learn some important techniques, it is not very probable that they will constitute a major part of your writing output.

The short-short can be a most effective way of telling a story consisting of an uncomplicated single incident with a surprise ending. It has to be of the kind which can be entered into without a build-up of any kind. Background and atmosphere are minimal, and the characters are one-dimensional with no other personality required other than to move the story quickly to that surprise at the end. This can be observed quite easily in this example:—

Clean out of clues

Detective Inspector Probend drove his car to the side of the alley and waited patiently for the covered lorry to pull away from the loading bank. Inside the warehouse a bright orange fork lift truck piled packing cases up to the roof. Beside him on the car seat lay a bulging case folder with burred edges.

Three days ago the Superintendent had given it to him with seven sheets of paper inside. Now it held over two hundred.

'Just a little job for you to sort out, Probend,' the Super said, 'a few washing machines gone astray.'

Probend didn't believe a word of it. He knew, and the Super knew, that he was never, ever, given a 'little job'.

11

A practised flick through the documents told him all that he needed to know for now. Thirty-two Dutch spin driers stolen from a store one night, eighteen months ago. Results of investigation – a blank.

'Where's the catch?' he asked.

The Superintendent glared, outraged for a moment, then gave a resigned shrug. 'If you care to go down to Documents Section, they'll give you another thirty folders just like that one,' he said. 'every job the same – perfect. All departmental or domestic equipment stores. All during the night, and never a sign of the stuff afterwards.'

Detective Inspector Probend was not a brilliant man. Neither was he a boastful man. But if he ever *was* to boast, it would be concerning the fact that he was not brilliant.

Brilliance he was content to leave to others.

Three days and three ounces of cut cavendish later, there were thirty empty case files and one splitting at the seams. Two hundred pages of what *was* known about the crimes and, in Probend's thick, deliberate writing, one page of what was *not* known.

Over and over he plodded through his list, eliminating each small mystery until only two remained. What happened to the loot from each raid? And why was none of it British made?

On the wall of his office hung a badly printed motto on plywood; a souvenir of a case that ended in Margate. DRIVE THE NAIL THAT WILL GO.

Drive the nail that will go. The only nail that would go out of these two was the last one – why were none of the goods made in Britain?

The thirty telephone calls that he made took all of one morning. Thirty different voices blended together in one common reply. Their goods had been supplied by the Britopean and Oriental Import Company – the same name which now peered at him from a crudely painted notice board hanging dangerously over the doorway.

Probend had an idea. Not brilliant, but an idea he had slogged for on his own.

Inside, the place was a warren of cardboard boxes; covered with unfamiliar manufacturer's names; Hitsukushi – Chang Foy – Carlovetti. All of these names appeared in his file.

He asked for and shook the hand of the managing director, Ferris. Probend came quickly to the point. 'Quite frankly, Mr Ferris,' he said, 'this gang has us completely puzzled.

Whoever is the top man must be a genius. And that's why I've come to you.'

Ferris accepted the compliment with a pleased smile. 'I always understood that the police knew a little bit about detection, Inspector,' he scoffed.

'What about clues? Surely they must have left some clues?'

'Not one, Mr Ferris. In fact, I'm almost beginning to believe that they take their own charlady with them.'

A laugh exploded from Ferris's lips. 'You mean to say that they break in, then sweep the floor?'

The inspector hid his embarrassment by examining a Japanese hair drier. 'Not only do they sweep the floor, Mr Ferris. On the last job they even took away the cardboard cases that the machines were delivered in. If there *are* any clues, they must have taken them with them.'

Once again Ferris laughed. 'You must excuse me, Inspector, but surely the answer is obvious. The goods must be disposed of in some way.'

'We've spent more than just a little time probing that,' Probend told him, 'and it's got us nowhere. As I said, the man's a genius.'

'I don't know about that,' Ferris said,' but he's certainly good for business.'

Probend cocked an enquiring eyebrow.

'Oh, yes, Inspector. Every time one of my customers gets raided, he has to restock. Right now I'm getting ready a batch of washing machines to replace the ones stolen last week.'

'I made a visit to the store yesterday,' Probend said. He went on: 'Do you know what depresses me about this case?'

'No, Inspector. What's that?'

'Here I am looking for washing machines, and I haven't the foggiest idea what they look like.'

Ferris beckoned him to come to the loading bay. 'We can soon fix that, Inspector. These are the ones that I'm going to deliver. Only came in today.'

Probend lifted the top flap of a large cardboard box. Inside stood the machine. He whistled admiringly at the quality, opened the lid and felt inside.

Ferris preened at the impression made by the washer. 'That's the best model on the market, and the cheapest,' he boasted. 'Anyone who buys one of those in the sale will get his real money's worth.'

'There's no doubt about that,' said Probend. 'Particularly

13

as he will be getting a free packet of washing powder inside.'

Probend drew his hand out of the machine holding a garishly coloured box. 'Just like this one, Mr Ferris. You see, the first thing the store did when the machines were delivered, was to put the washing powder in. You and your gang didn't leave any clues, Mr Ferris. But you certainly brought a giant-size one away with you.'

Reprinted by permission of Fact & Fiction Agency.

As we mentioned earlier, there is little time in which to develop character in the short-short story. The Superintendent is a nothing. Of Ferris we can only guess that he is cheeky and somewhat self-assured. Probend we see as a pipesmoking and dedicated plodder, perhaps in his fifties, and perhaps just a little craftier than would appear on the surface. Although every story, so we are told, should have an element of clash or conflict, in this case it is very low-key. The nub of the story is the reversal of a villain leaving a clue at the scene of the crime. Just that one incident, and little else besides.

Chapter Two

HUMOUR

From what has been said so far, it is relatively easy to define a short story with a fair degree of accuracy. The same can be said of the humorous piece, although it is not so readily obvious.

You will sometimes see a published humorous article or essay, but these are rare indeed. What you will more often see is a humorous piece which closely follows the recipe given for the short-short story – a single incident with a surprise ending. So, although this book does not set out to cover humour in great detail, it is worth a mention to the new writer so that he can appreciate that mastering the form of the short story has other advantages. We must also mention that the humorist has a larger cross to bear than the writer of short stories. Humour is a very individual thing. What causes one editor to pop some buttons will cause another to yawn his head off. To make the point of the humorous piece comparing closely with any short story, we reproduce an example. It has been published, but it will not amuse every reader – tastes in humour being what they are.

The big toe

Isn't pain awful! It's so ... so ... well, it's so painful, to say the least. And when pain gets the bit between its teeth and dashes off in all directions at once, then it becomes agony.

My neighbour, Fred, took up with agony a little while ago. In his foot. Shooting pains. First they started. Then they stopped. Then they started – these shooting pains – to start and stop, non-stop.

Poor Fred! Every time the shooting stopped, it was only a temporary lull in the attack until the next ammunition train arrived.

I saw him the other day. I could see that he was in agony because of the agonised expression on his face. And the crutches propping him up. And his foot all bandaged up like a mummified marrow.

As is my wont, I thought to myself, 'My goodness! Tut-Tut! Bless my soul!' and various other strong expressions of surprise and concern. So, I walked up to him – very lively and chirpy, and said, 'Hello, Fred! Putting your best foot forward, I see!'

Now, after I picked myself up from the pavement, he told me where his agony had decided to set itself up in permanent residence. And that was his big toe.

I don't know if you have kept yourself informed of these matters, but our big toe happens to be one of the two most sensitive parts of the body. The other big toe is the other one.

I can hear you clamouring for substantiative evidence. You shall have it in abundance.

You must have heard of these dreadful Chinese doctor chaps who push horrid long needles into poor suffering people. That's it – acupuncturists. A longish name and a trifle inconvenient for the average sized visiting card I would have thought, but one well worth while getting on speaking terms with. Then you won't make the mistake of ordering one with your chow mein and sweet and sour.

These acupuncturists say that there is a nerve in the big toe which travels all the way up to your forehead. That is if it is *your* big toe we are talking about. Naturally, if it is the other fellow's big toe, it will have the entrée to *his* forehead.

I suppose that is why, when we bang our big toe, we tend to go crosseyed. Yes, it apparently is all one big nerve. And what goes in one end must come out of the other.

I mentioned this to Fred, and suggested that the big toe was really trying to tell him that a new pair of spectacles would not come amiss. But no, Fred had just bought some, and they were quite satisfactory except for the small fortune he was charged for them. An accurate diagnosis, as he saw it, was rheumatism, sciatica, arthritis, lumbosis, gout and more than a fair helping of molten lead. All mixed with just a soupçon of torture to hold it together.

Now, it just happens that my Grannie used to have a bad toe, on and off. And sometimes she couldn't kick a football for days on end.

At first, she would go to bed and put her feet on Grandpa. A sort of reverse laying on of hands. Then Grandpa claimed

16

that he had caught this malady off her in his back. He bought himself another bed, and she bought herself a great stone hot water bottle. She said that the bottle was better than Grandpa, anyway — and she wished the devil she had met it before she met him. Grandpa said so did he — so the incident didn't cause any disagreement.

I still had this hot water bottle, and I told Fred that he was welcome to borrow it. And he did.

I must confess that I had completely and utterly forgotten the problem that she had with it. You see, it is very, very heavy. And after a few hours of roasting comfort, it goes into reverse gear and becomes a most efficient refrigeration plant. It is certainly not to be trusted. Doze off and you are likely to wake up as a mammoth in an ice-berg with the primroses still blooming in your mouth. You have to keep one jump ahead of it all the time.

Grannie used to control the situation by kicking it out of bed just as she began to smell the scent of primroses. Usually about midnight. We became quite used to the thundering crashes after a while. And it stopped coming through the ceiling, once we covered her floor with corrugated iron sheets.

In bed that night, I remembered that I should have told Fred how to handle the brute. But suddenly, on the stroke of midnight, there came a familiar and horrendous crash from next door. After climbing back into bed, I realised that Fred must have now worked out the strategy for himself.

The next morning, Fred caught up with me on the way to the station. What a fantastic change in a man! No more crutches. Not the slightest sign of a limp on any part of his body. I was so pleased for him.

But!

It seems that he had been staggering up the stairs with this great bottle on his back, and he missed the top stair. The crash I heard must have been him hitting his head on the way down.

And miracle of all miracles! The pain in his toe vanished in one blinding flash. The big nerve phenomenon, you see. His toe was reborn. He was a new man.

Mind you, the great blue throbbing lump between his eyes was giving him agony. But, that's life. What you win on the swings, you sometimes lose on the roundabouts.

One must be prepared to be philosophical about miracles.

Reprinted by permission of Fact & Fiction Agency.

You should be able to recognise the short-short story principles in this piece. The incident is the history of the hot water bottle, and the surprise is at the end. Nearly all of the characterisation in the story is invested in the person telling the story, but Grannie, Grandpa and Fred are given just enough of a dimension to fit them into the life of the story-teller.

Time and time again the Greek philosophers of yesteryear say that life is a mixture of drama and comedy. And so it is. Unless you have spent your last twenty-four hours locked privately in your room, with no reading, listening or viewing facilities available to you, then you surely will have had moments which were more dramatic than others. You will also have had moments which were more humorous than others. We do not mean moments of great dramatic impact, nor times when you laughed yourself into tears. We are talking of balance – the highs and lows of ordinary living are not extremes, but we experience them all the time. We take them for granted, and if we do not get our fair share, then we sometimes go looking for them. Have you ever watched a bored child kept inactive by sickness or inclement weather? That child will soon start to 'look for trouble' as it is often described.

Even the dullest life will tend to have its moments of drama and comedy.

There could be many, many reasons why a person would read fiction – in the present case the short story. But most of them would stem from the reader's basic desire to somehow experience life to a greater degree by sharing in the joys and woes of others – even if they are fictional characters. His own personal circumstances may only permit him to cross the English Channel by Hovercraft a few times during his life. But by reading, he can sail around the world a thousand times.

It has been said before that if visitors from another planet returned home and reported that the inhabitants of Earth spent a considerable amount of their time both telling and listening to lies, then they may have a hard time making themselves believed.

The skilled writer of fiction writes lies dressed up as truth. He understands that his reader is looking for more than his own life affords him in the way of drama and comedy. The story is made more interesting than ordinary everyday events present themselves to the reader. *But not to the extent that the lie becomes too much to swallow.*

It is obvious that the reader has both a motive and an expectation when picking up a short story. His prime motive is to add to his life experience – albeit through the actions of fictional characters. And

18

his expectation is that the experiences of these fictional characters will, in the main, be more dramatic and humorous than those he experiences during his everyday living. Both the dramatic and humorous aspects of fiction have to be selective and highlighted to fill the reader's appetite. The lies must be interesting and concentrated lies, which stop short of the unbelievable.

This is why humour has been introduced so early in this book. It goes hand in hand with the dramatic.

You should stop reading for a moment and recall the dirtiest villain that has appeared in your life. Not a fictional character, but somebody, perhaps, who has given you a bad time. If you are honest, you will probably admit that the person, no matter how bad, had at least one redeeming and good aspect of character. The maiden aunt who always corrected you before company may have given wonderful birthday and Christmas presents. The boss who treated you like a slave and paid a higher salary than you ever earned before, and even introduced you to his daughter before you took fright and ran. Few are the villains who are 100% nitric acid.

Similarly, you may have some hero that you almost worship, to the point of being able to avoid looking at his or her faults completely. Once again, if you are totally honest, you would agree that your hero to some degree has feet of clay.

Real live people are neither exclusively saint or devil, but some mixture of both. Your reader knows this – he sees evidence around him every day that he lives in the company of others. He would not reasonably expect to find and recognise these positive and minus aspects of character from one brief and casual meeting with a stranger. But he would expect to know and understand the person better as the relationship grew. When he had spent more time with the person.

This is another factor of reality which an author must allow for in his fictional work. In a novel, novella, or the longer type of short story, the reader is spending more time with the character in the story, and can reasonably expect to get to know him better. Without, perhaps, realising it, the reader will be looking for evidence of the character's worth. And if the author portrays that character as *completely* saint or devil, then the reader will feel vaguely suspicious that he is being sold something which is just too good or too bad to be true. The longer you leave your fictional character in the company of your reader, the more you should reveal the soul of that fictional character – not forgetting the other side of the coin.

So far, we have been addressing ourselves to the short short story. At 1,750 words or so, the characters in the story pop up before the reader and are gone within a moment. They are mere puppets constructed to portray the incident which is a lie on the part of the author in order to amuse the reader. The reader can not and would expect not to know the personality traits of a real live person during such a brief encounter. Neither does he expect to understand the inner workings of a fictional character in this manner. So, we can now make a definite statement about characters appearing in the short short story.

No characters in the short short story need to be portrayed in any more depth than is necessary to describe the *incident*.

This little rule should not be undervalued just because it is a little rule. Grasping it is, in fact, the first step in the direction of writing a saleable short short story. The telling of a story within the limits of 1,750 words means that hardly a word can be wasted. The reader does not expect to know the characters in any depth, so don't waste words. Use them all for telling the *story*. And this rule only applies to the *short short story*, as will be explained later.

Chapter Three

CAUSE AND EFFECT

Before we go any further with our close look at the structure of the short story, let us take a look at the structure of any kind of fictional story in general terms.

We have already indicated that a reader could turn to fiction because he finds life in real terms lacking in drama and comedy. Not just through boredom, but positively, because he wishes to extend his experience — even second-hand and in imagination.

Each of us would probably admit that our life so far has been one long (or not so long) series of causes and effects. As cause, you put a coin in a machine, and the effect is that something comes out of the machine. With the advent of the tea and coffee machine, we must qualify that statement by saying that you put a coin in a tea and coffee machine and *hope* that something will come out!

But if you think over carefully some of these cause and effect cycles which you have experienced then, interestingly enough, many of the effects are, in fact, causes which produce further effects. If one takes this to the extreme, it would be easy to convince yourself that somehow you had been born into a stream of cause and effect over which you had no control. A number of people will use this as an excuse for their unsuccessful lives.

The average human being gets great satisfaction out of recognising causes and effects. When we were young our elders certainly seemed to derive great satisfaction from telling us that our problems were our own fault — we caused the effect. Similarly, the reader gets an equal amount of satisfaction from being able to identify cause and effect in fiction. He prefers to start with a cause and end with a definite effect.

There is another golden rule which stands out two miles high. It applies to any form of fiction – not just to the short story. Causes which have an effect on the main character should, usually, be bad effects. Any effects brought about or caused by the main character should, usually, be the good effects of the story.

Now, this may seem to be quite complicated, but let us take an example.

We begin a story with our main character or hero in a pickle or with a problem. The story deals with *his* handling of the problem, or what *he* does to get out of the pickle. Let us suppose that we first meet him in a state of financial ruin. He and his business partner borrowed a huge sum of money for their business. They have both put up as guarantee everything that they possess. Now both the partner and the money are missing.

The effect is that our hero faces bankruptcy. The cause was the disappearance of the partner with the money. Without another factor coming into the story, the ending is quite obvious. If the story is to continue and be interesting, there must be another cause leading to another effect. This is called plot development. This next cause will be initiated by the hero himself, or by some outside agency. If you want the story to develop, then any cause from an outside agency must lead to a *bad* effect on the hero. Any good effect will pull your story to a halt. If the partner reappears with the money there is no more story. If the bank is lenient there is no story. And if the hero wins the football pools there is no story. If the hero is going to make any headway at all out of the problem, then he must cause it himself with little or no help from anyone else. If he is married, then it is permissible for his wife to help him because, for the purpose of this story we can treat them as one person sharing exactly the same problem.

You should also remember that effects are usually more interesting than causes. Starting your story by giving the detailed description of the cause is usually pretty dreary, and this is a main reason why so many written pieces fail to make any impact on a reader.

Let us say that you are writing a story about Molly losing her job. Obviously, losing her job is the effect of some cause. More often than not, the cause of her losing her job will be quite unimportant to the story. You can ignore it completely or just cover it in a few words. If the cause of her losing her job *is* important to the story, then the facts should be covered later in the story.

Let us take an example of each type of beginning, starting with the cause.

(Cause) Molly had worked at Habkins Engineering Works

since she left school five years ago. They were good employers and Molly had been quite happy with them working in the accounts department. All of the staff knew that the firm was facing severe financial problems. Overtime was a thing of the past, and the monthly bonus had shrunk to almost nothing. There had been rumours over the past few weeks that staff cuts were now a distinct possibility. But with only one other girl working with her in accounts, Molly felt her job was as safe as houses. So, it came as an enormous shock to her when she was told that her employment had, regrettably, come to an end.

You see, when you want to write about a cause, you have to spell it out in some detail, and this will slow the beginning of your story. You cannot avoid it.

Let us now leave aside the cause of Molly losing her job and begin with the effect itself.

(Effect) Molly came out of the director's office with a dry mouth. Her hand shook as she closed the door, and she hardly heard the voice calling after her that she could have an excellent reference. Molly was sacked. Habkins Engineering just couldn't afford her any more.

By starting with an effect, you move straight into the story without any delay, and you give the reader a question to hold on to for a moment. And that is always a good way to hold attention and create a desire to know more.

If you wish, you can plan your whole story out in the form of a map before you begin to write it, by making a list of cause, effect, cause, effect and so on. Always remembering to start with an effect.

There is another aspect of the cause and effect equation which can be most important, particularly when you are writing the longer and more fleshed out kind of short story. You will sometimes need to use an effect which is sensational to some degree. Possibly something which is quite outrageous and highly dramatic. In these instances you are duty bound to explain this large effect with a very reasonable cause.

Taking Molly again, we shall say that she has a close friend who we shall call Jan. From the beginning of the story, we see that they get along very well together. Now, for some reason of your own choosing, you wish there to be a clash between them of quite large proportions. You are in your best trouble-making form as you are

23

writing, and you intend that Jan should make your day by throwing a glass of water into Molly's face. If you want to maintain any kind of reality in your story for the reader, then you must justify this large effect by just as large a cause. It is expected in real life terms and is just as expected in fiction for the intelligent reader. There is really no great problem to sorting this one out. All you should do is to ask yourself just what somebody would have to do to *you* to make you want to douse them with cold water. Satisfy yourself that it is a reasonable explanation, then type it onto the paper.

Chapter Four

CHARACTER

All of your stories will be concerned with people. And people come in all sorts of shapes, sizes, colours and degrees of pleasantness. Each of them has a particular character, just as people do in real life. And it is character which will concern you, the writer, more than any other aspect of fiction writing. So, as we now wish to keep the idea of character and characterisation very much in mind, we shall no longer refer to the persons appearing in fiction than by any other name than — characters.

The first thing you should learn is that you never, ever tell the reader about your characters, *you let him see them in action*. If you wish your reader to intensely dislike Jacob Gronk, don't bother to give your reasons — just show Jacob Gronk stomping along the street, then stopping briefly to kick a kitten over the wall.

In case you didn't notice, there were actually three items of characterisation in that last sentence. The name — Jacob Gronk, the fact that he was 'stomping' along the street, and his unforgivable action of kicking a tiny, cuddly creature over a wall.

Just change these three items of characterisation, and you get a quite different effect. Peter Noble strolls along the street, then stops to kick away a mangey cur which is snapping at the ankles of a young mother who is pushing her pram.

There is no plot so far in these examples of different types of character, and that is something which you are advised to think over and digest. *Well presented characters are ninety percent of the story*. No matter how new you are to the game of writing, you can take any one of these two characters and continue along a similar course with some conflicts and problems, and finish up with some kind of interesting story. Then, if you read it, you will find that you have constructed a plot. To be more precise, *you* didn't construct a plot, the characters did.

Well constructed characters and a strong plot are essential for a good story, but the characters are far, far more important.

We just used the term 'well constructed characters'. What we mean by this is that you, the author, are in the god-like position of tailor-making characters to be and perform in any way that you choose. It is really quite amusing to listen to an author (even an experienced one) saying that the story will not work because a character is 'wrong'. Why doesn't he just abandon that unsuitable character and create one which is 'right'? There is nothing sacred about story characters, they are designed to serve a function and nothing more. We occasionally come upon a so-called author who has very strange ideas and attitudes about his writings. He makes up all kinds of ridiculous conventions and obligations for himself and his work for no good reasons that seem sensible to the sane person.

The greatest skill demanded of an author is to create seemingly *real* characters which react reasonably to what is going on about them in the story. This does not mean that every character must be predictable or sane, but the behaviour and reaction must be based on reality. In the book, TREASURE ISLAND, we meet an old castaway by the name of Ben Gunn. There can be no description of him other than that he is a crazy old coot, who has been both alone and out in the sun far too long. But the author, R. L. Stevenson, has constructed Ben Gunn so cleverly that we are obliged to accept him as behaving quite reasonably within his own insane framework.

There are, supposedly, only 36 basic plots which may be constructed, but characters are in an endless supply. As Somerset Maugham once said; 'The only subject which is inexhaustible is man'.

Earlier on, we mentioned the equation of cause and effect. Now that we have introduced the additional factor of character, we can ask *who* caused it and *who* did it affect? And not only who, but *how*? The how depends on the who, and the who depends on who the author created.

Events in your story are only as important as the characters they affect. If the characters seem unreal to the reader, then the reader will not care a fig for what is happening. What you must remember is that the events and what results from the events must be of the greatest importance to the main characters in the story.

If you keep your eyes open in the second-hand book shops, you will sometimes come across collections of short stories published in the 1930's. You will usually find that these fall into distinct categories of detective, adventure, mystery and humour. It will be of great benefit to you to study these works. You just have to remember that you are reading excellent examples of *how not to do it*. The 1930's was a period when a great deal of awful short stories were published. Successful publishers are only as successful as the works they select and publish are bought by the public. So we can only assume that public taste at that time differed enormously from that of today. The bulk of these works can be described as frivolous and trivial. The characters were usually middle or upper-class twits, who invariably destroyed perfectly good story plots with their ridiculous behaviour. They took nothing seriously, unless it happened to be affairs of their tennis club or some chocolate box flapper by the name of Toodles, usually with a father of Colonel Blimp countenance and gouty disposition.

You may take it as the gospel truth that today publishers of all lengths of story get their regular share of submitted material which is straight out of the 1930's. It is quite unusable.

At the time of writing of this book, there was a current film being shown called BEYOND THE POISEDON ADVENTURE. A young woman and her father are escaping from a burning and sinking ship which has turned turtle on the high seas. The girl sees her father gunned down with machine gun bullets. She is most suitably distressed and weeps over his still and bloody body. She then climbs an upside-down steel ladder to another deck where she immediately gets involved in the 'adventure' concerning gold coins — all thoughts of her father now completely gone from her mind. Perhaps it was necessary for the pace of the film to be maintained, but the scriptwriter certainly didn't do much for the reality of the character. He could at least have her recover from her bereavement over the course of a minute or so. It is small slips like this in fiction which stand out in great starkness and destroy believable characterisation.

You will appreciate that story telling is aimed at the emotions of the reader, not to his intellect. It is quite possible that the author may have some significant 'message' that he wishes to share with the world. He may wish to change human values, politics, religions, ethics or anything else under the sun. If he is writing factual material, then he will aim for the intellect and conscious mind of his reader. But if he elects to employ fiction to convey his ideas then he must initially reach the heart of his reader through the emotional route.

The average human being is far, far more open to emotional effects than he or she would ever dare admit to publicly. Even the most hard-hearted of us can be caught off our guard at times. To some, it may be from hearing LAND OF HOPE AND GLORY played by massed bands. To others, it may be from pictures of pathetic children hardly surviving in some banana dictatorship. Others yet, are moved by wedding ceremonies, public speakers or even receiving a kind word or gift from an unexpected source. All such responses are emotional. After the event we could look back and ask ourselves why on earth we reacted in such a way.

You have to remember that in fiction, you are reaching the emotions of the reader via the emotions and behaviour of one or more characters – not the events. You may read a factual account of some disaster that takes place on the opposite side of the world from you. You may be impressed with the cold factual account. But, subconsciously, you are very much aware that the event is taking place at a very safe distance from you. It is not *your* problem. But, let some writer who is gifted at playing on your raw nerve endings give you an account of the disaster in the *human* terms of suffering or bravery and you may not find it so easy to get to sleep at night. He will have given you the reality of the situation. To be effective, fiction also has to carry the same convincing reality. Be it high comedy, or the most harrowing of dramas, it must seem to concern real people.

Chekhov said, 'Avoid depicting the hero's state of mind; you ought to make it clear from the hero's actions.'

This is the soundest of advice to the pupil writer. In real life terms, you do not have some disembodied spirit standing at your shoulder telling you what is going on in other people's minds. You have learned to use your eyes and ears and work it out for yourself. And, if you are more than two years old, you are most likely doing a pretty fine job of it. For you, that is what real life is all about. You expect to figure out your fellow human beings for yourself. And, if you have had your fingers burned a few times from listening to gossip – why should you listen to someone else's opinion of another when you can do a far better job yourself? Your reader is accustomed to using his common sense in real life terms. Just give him a really good character in operation, and you will rarely have to do any mind reading stunts for him.

Slightly to recap what we have said so far; the amount of words available to you in your story will determine how much you can give to building of believable character. In the short-short story, you must get by with just two-dimensional characters. You must make every word count.

One very basic and simple way is to include subtle characterisation over and above the actual words that your character uses.

'You will never get to the other side alive,' Henry said.

For the same number of words, you can give the *manner* or the emotional content of them.

'You will never get to the other side alive,' Henry sneered.
'You will never get to the other side alive,' Henry grinned.
'You will never get to the other side alive,' Henry wailed.
'You will never get to the other side alive,' Henry sighed.
'You will never get to the other side alive,' Henry gasped.

Quite obviously, Henry is a man of many parts. But, if you carry on with all the variations of 'Henry said' throughout your story, it will all become very dull and predictable. So, you ring the changes, each time giving an indicator to Henry's character.

Henry yawned. 'You'll never get to the other side.'
Henry wiped his mouth. 'You'll never get to the other side.'
Henry's eyes popped. 'You'll never get to the other side.'
Henry spoke slowly. 'You'll never get to the other side.'

Where you have the words to spare, and that certainly will not be in the short-short story, you can add to Henry's character build-up with almost every piece of dialogue he makes.

Henry looked her up and down disdainfully. 'You'll never get to the other side.'

Henry let the clutch slip in, and called over his shoulder. 'You'll never get to the other side.'

Henry pulled back his balled fist, his face a mask of fury. 'You'll never get to the other side.'

The match shook as Henry lit the cigarette. 'You'll never get to the other side.'

Henry slapped the old dog's head as he coaxed her away from the reeds. 'You'll never get to the other side,' he laughed.

'You'll ... you'll ...' Henry paused, then spluttered in his high-pitched voice, 'you'll never get to the other side.'

This far, we have only slightly scratched the surface of characterisation. It is a subject on which a writer can seem to learn more for ever. But, the little you now have will help you to write stories which seem to concern real people.

Chapter Five

CHARACTER IN ACTION

You can never learn enough about characterisation. You can never *write* enough. Whenever you read a short story written by another, you should always study how the author does it. If the story is your own copy, you should underline in coloured ink or pencil those aspects of character that you believe are particularly well presented. So, take up your coloured pencil and mark up the following story.

The Con

Frank Cobb drank the medicine and returned the glass to the waiting nurse. He peered closely at her slim white figure. He grudgingly preferred this one to the other two that Dr. Wise sent along. Too bossy by far they were, and each of them only lasted until they removed his cigars and lighter from the side of his bed. The second one even did so with the objection that they were dangerous to *her* health. Blasted woman! She could go some place else, and he hoped she picked up a germ that would teach her a lesson. But this one was of a different breed. Slim, without being scrawny, and certainly no more than forty-five years old. She came the day before yesterday and hadn't yet tried her strength with him. Most likely she was waiting her opportunity. Waiting until she could be in the right and have him in the wrong. But she didn't seem the type who would be trivial. That's it, just waiting for an opportunity.

'I'm going to smoke a cigar,' he growled.

She took the dirty glass to the bathroom, calling over her shoulder, 'I was just going to give you a bed-bath, Mr. Cobb.'

'I'm going to have a smoke. Don't you hear so well?'

From where he lay in the bed he could see her rinse the glass, wipe it dry and put it with all of the other damned paraphernalia they kept out there for him. As she came back into the room, he jammed a long, slim Schimmelpenninck into his mouth, lit it and blew a challenging jet of smoke at the ceiling.

'That smells nice,' she said quietly. 'We'll leave the bath until you've finished it.'

So, this one played the game by a different set of rules, did she? Treat him like a baby so that he wouldn't cause her any bother. He watched her writing in that blasted book they kept well away from his sight. She was calmly ignoring that he was doing his health no good at all by filling his lungs with foul smoke. She was not living up to the standards that her job demanded. She was taking his money under false pretences.

He glared at her sternly over his spectacles. 'Dr. Wise says I shouldn't be using these stinking things.'

'Yes, that's what he told me,' she smiled.

'So, it's your job to report it. That's what you're paid for.'

She returned the pen to her breast pocket. 'I've just written it in the book, Mr Cobb.'

'Show me,' he growled. 'Show me what you've said about me.'

She held the book open before him. The entry was no more than an inch long. '10 a.m. Cigar.' It carried no impact, no emphasis, no personal involvement. She had passed the buck to Dr. Wise to handle and, goddamit, what he said about cigars was of no importance at all. His attitude towards her would need a rethink to some extent. She wore a wedding ring, so she could have been more tamed down than the other two biddies.

'You're the first nurse I've had who was a maried woman,' he said. 'If your husband's a smoker, he can have some of these. I'm going to give them up soon.'

'Thank you, Mr Cobb, but my husband died a year ago,' she said quietly.

'I'm sorry to hear that,' he said. 'I suppose you were a nurse before you married.'

'Quite a long time ago, actually,' she said. And he was sure he saw a laugh in her eyes. 'But it's like swimming, you never forget how to be a nurse, because patients never change.' She tapped one of his feet lightly. 'Your toe-nails are far too long, Mr Cobb. I should like to trim them please.'

'I'm smoking,' he reminded her sharply.

31

'Quite a few men do when they are at the chiropodist,' she said as she pulled back the bedclothes at the bottom of the bed. She sat down and took a small pair of scissors from her pocket, and examined his feet. 'That's a very large corn you have. Does it bother you?'

'Only when I walk, so it doesn't matter.'

'Right, then we'll do something about it. We'll see if we can clear it up by the time you are on your feet again.'

Oh, Lord! Here was another one who was going to try and maintain the fiction that there was much more life ahead of him. He knew better than any of them that it was a lie. He was worn out at sixty. The little tape recorder which started when he was conceived, and built and rebuilt his body over the years, was coming to its end. The recording of Frank Cobb was nearly over. And there were no buttons which could be pressed to rewind and replay a single minute more. Not that he had any complaints with the programme. He just didn't like to see others kidding themselves, even if they tried to kid him.

Change the subject. 'So you've come back to nurse private patients?'

She shortened two nails with deft snips. 'It's what seems to suit me best,' she said. 'For a little while I worked in a psychiatric ward, but that was a mistake.'

'The whole damned psychiatric thing is a mistake, if you ask me,' he growled. 'All those millions being spent to make sick people worse, and the world doesn't even lift an eyebrow. Try that in any other business, and you would go to jail.'

'Oh, it isn't quite that bad,' she said. 'Something has to be done to help these poor people. You just can't ignore their suffering.'

'Then give them a proper medical examination. The chances are that they are physically sick. Going out of their minds with pain, some of them. I had an aunt once who nearly sent the whole family crazy with her tantrums. When I heard they had a shrink lined up licking his lips with a nice sharp ice-pick ready to poke into her brain, I took her off to a sane doctor. All she had was a crazy gall bladder. It went – and so did her madness.'

She turned her attention to his other foot. 'It would be a great mistake to judge psychiatry by the one example.'

'One example – hell!' Cobb exploded. 'Do you know that a survey was taken in the States some years ago? What percentage of mental patients having psychiatric treatment recovered compared with those who had no treatment at all? Can you guess the result?'

'I had better not guess,' she said. 'Because I have a strong feeling, from the tone of your voice, that it isn't going to be good.'

'Twenty percent having treatment showed a noticeable improvement. And twenty-five percent having no attention at all eventually got over it. Depending on how you juggle the figures, you could read that as saying if you dumped all the trick-cyclists in the Pacific, then twenty more cases out of every hundred would get themselves cured up just fine.' He spluttered and coughed with the exertion and jammed out the cigar in the ashtray.

The nurse stood up and put away the scissors. 'Well, at least we know how you feel about psychiatrists,' she said calmly. 'And now that you've finished your smoke, we'll get on with your bed-bath.' She returned to the bathroom for the washing things and called. 'But psychology isn't all bad, you know.'

He raised himself on one elbow and glared at her. 'My good woman, I am not talking about psychology. I am talking about psychiatrists – the hatchet men of the medical profession.'

She returned with a bowl of warm water and placed it down beside the bed. 'All right, then. We'll drop the psychiatrists and the psychologists in the Pacific for the moment,' she laughed as she unbuttoned his pyjama jacket.

'Perhaps some of the psychologists,' he said, simmering down. 'But not all of them. There is at least one who deserves better than that.'

'Would I have heard of him?'

'No,' he said as she lathered his chest gently. 'He was an old Buddhist priest I met in India more than thirty years ago. Now, there was a man who knew what he was talking about.'

'Well, Mr Cobb,' she said. 'For you to say that, he must have made quite an impression on you. I hope it turned out to be to your advantage.'

'That it certainly was,' he grinned. 'I'm quite a wealthy man, and I have something of a reputation in the business world. Do you know what that reputation is?'

'I have no idea, Mr Cobb. Now, please turn over and let me wash your back.'

He rolled over onto his belly and relaxed. 'I'm known as the man who can do the impossible. Although that doesn't happen to be strictly true. The people who work for me do that, and I pay them well for it. I motivate them. And how do you suppose that I motivate them?'

'Well, you just said that you pay them well.'

'That's not motivation, that's reward,' he chuckled.

'For all I know, perhaps you threaten them.'

He turned his head and frowned at her. 'What do you take me for — a damned psychiatrist? No, I motivate them with hope and white lies. That's what I learned from that old Buddhist priest. I decide what the world needs in the way of a new product, then tell my people to get on with it.'

'Well, Mr Cobb, if you don't mind me saying so, that doesn't sound like very much motivation.'

'Ahah!' he laughed. 'But I tell them to do the impossible.'

'Oh, really!' she said in disbelief. 'How on earth can anyone do the impossible?'

'Because I tell them that someone else has already done it. I tell them that our competitors have come up with something secret, and I've been tipped off. I don't even ask them if we can do it. I just ask if we can come out with our version first. And it works every time. My people do well out of it. I do well out of it. And the whole damned world does well out of that little white lie. I suppose you will want to make some objection to that.'

'No, I have no objection. In fact, I think that what you are doing is quite wonderful. And you really must get well soon and get back to do some more.'

Oh, God! Here it was again! The same old hogwash about recovering his youth and getting back on his feet again. He expected better from her than that. She was expecting him to do the impossible. 'Nuts!' he said sourly.

'Now you shouldn't say that, Mr Cobb. You may be very clever, but you don't know everything. I happen to be in a far better position to make a judgement on your state of health than you do.'

'Bah!' he grunted. 'Have you ever seen anyone in my condition make a complete recovery?'

'I certainly have — many times. In fact, the last of them that I nursed is now in his grandchildren's baseball team,' she laughed.

'It's no joking matter,' he said, now sadly.

34

'But I'm not joking, Mr Cobb — it happens to be quite true. The medicine that you drank a few minutes ago is working miracles for people with your condition. And even though you choose not to believe it, Dr Wise is considered to be one of the leading authorities. You will just have to face up to the fact that you are going to get well. And there is absolutely nothing you can do to prevent it from happening. Tomorrow morning, I am going to help you walk to the bathroom.'

He shook his head slowly. 'I'll never make it.'

'Oh, but you will, Mr Cobb, there's no doubt about it. The medicine will make sure of that. We just don't know how long it will take you. Now, I'll just change this water, and then we'll wash your legs for tomorrow's outing.'

She went again to the bathroom, humming quietly as she emptied the bowl and ran fresh water. He looked at her steadily as she stood there, a figure of calm confidence. Then he threw back his head and hooted with laughter. The confounded woman was using his own technique on himself. Not only was she insisting that he could do it, but she was bringing in the time factor as he always did with his people. Godammit — why not! It always worked for him, so why not for her? She deserved to pull it off. She could treat an old coot like himself with respect and still stay on equal terms. And when you took a real close look at her, she was really quite a dish. Getting back to good health was beginning to look like a pretty interesting proposition!

Reprinted by permission of Fact & Fiction Agency.

The plot content of this short story is really quite small. It is based on Jacob Cobb conning his workers and the nurse conning him in the same fashion. There is also his criticism of psychiatrists in general terms. It so happens that the author of the story has a similar opinion of psychiatrists, so to some extent, it is a 'message'. But the reason for including it in the story was to give an opportunity for Jacob Cobb to 'act out a part' and reveal his character. It is also an associated lead-in to the subject of the old Buddhist priest.

If the author has done his work effectively, you should now have a mental picture of the patient and the nurse. You should know them as characters. And the author virtually told you nothing about either of them. They acted out a situation for you, and you drew your own conclusions.

It is also worth mentioning that in this particular short story, the

35

author has not attempted to build an 'atmosphere'. Nor has he described in any detail the place in which the action occurred. It has all been done by the characters 'acting'.

And, referrring to what was said earlier in this book about cause and effect — it started with an effect — a man was sick in bed. You were not given the cause — the nature of the illness. Perhaps he was suffering from a stroke, a heart attack or anything else. It really is of no importance. What *is* important is that these characters performed in the only possible way that these particular characters could in a certain situation.

Chapter Six

THIRTY-SIX SITUATIONS

If you have not already done so, you will surely come across the name of Georges Polti during your writing career. Polti is distinguished for his work in isolating and naming the thirty-six basic dramatic situations. Just as with ghosts and extra-terrestrial visitors, it seems that most of us have heard of him but never actually seen his work ourselves. It is therefore worth listing his thirty-six situations here so that you will not have to go hunting through dusty old tomes yourself.

First Situation – Supplication
Second Situation – Deliverance
Third Situation – Crime Pursued by Vengeance
Fourth Situation – Vengeance Taken for Kindred Upon Kindred
Fifth Situation – Pursuit
Sixth Situation – Disaster
Seventh Situation – Falling Prey to Cruelty or Misfortune
Eighth Situation – Revolt
Ninth Situation – Daring Enterprise
Tenth Situation – Abduction
Eleventh Situation – The Enigma
Twelfth Situation – Obtaining
Thirteenth Situation – Enmity of Kinsmen
Fourteenth Situation – Rivalry of Kinsmen
Fifteenth Situation – Murderous Adultery
Sixteenth Situation – Madness
Seventeenth Situation – Fatal Imprudence
Eighteenth Situation – Involuntary Crimes of Love
Nineteenth Situation – Slaying of a Kinsman Unrecognised
Twentieth Situation – Self-Sacrifice for an Ideal
Twenty-First Situation – Self-Sacrifice for Kindred

You should remember that Polti has given us these *situations*. They are not *plots*. Plots are developed from situations. And that is where the hard work and need for imagination comes in for you the writer.

These situations are very, very basic and will not immediately leap out to you from the printed page. To some extent, you have to learn to live with them, mull them over in your mind and define and develop more subtle situations before you can develop a plot.

For example, the thirteenth situation gives Enmity of Kinsmen. Taken too literally, this can only mean that there is bitterness and perhaps violence between members of the same family. You have to realise that enmity has a very wide range of meaning. It can be hostility, antagonism, opposition, unfriendliness, incompatibility, antipathy, loathing, dislike, hatred, animosity, spitefulness, grudgingness, ill-feeling, ill-will, jealousy, envy, coolness, estrangement, alienation, bitterness, rancour or many other kinds of negative affinity. You may, at first, feel that dealing with enmity is going to give you some pretty heavy dramatic material. Yet, most good comedy material has a strong element of enmity in it in one form or another. What is more, whatever the kind of enmity is involved, there is the aspect of 'volume' to be considered. Is it of a high volume, such as a world war? Or, is it of a slightly lower volume, such as a wife telling her husband that he has left off the cap of the tooth paste again?

Nor should the term 'kinsman' be taken to mean only the immediate members of a family. It is far, far better to assume that there is some degree of *relationship* between your characters.

Polti gave his definitions to writers as an aid, not to bind them with restraints, but to help them to help themselves. Seen in this light, the author will realise that the framework of thirty-six situations have been rendered down into a managable size to discuss as author to author, and *not to work with*.

It will also be found that the longer the work, the more probably that there is more than one situation in a story. As a rule of thumb, and not a rule of cast-iron, you should generally have one definite situation in a story which dominates any other situations. This will be quite obvious if we assume that you are going to write a longish short story concerning a group of six soldiers who are escaping from a prisoner of war camp. Presumably you will select one basic situation that you wish to develop. It may be the Twenty-First Situation: Self-Sacrifice for Kindred. You may wish to have one of them give up his life or liberty in order that the others may escape. If you give too much of your words to subsidiary situations (which you are obliged to include) then you will not have enough to accomplish your main purpose. For example, you would not bother too much with the Second Situation – Deliverance. You would not feel that several anti-climatic pages at the end should deal with the soldiers returning to their own group and their celebrations.

You should also bear in mind that Polti's situations are for your inspiration and guidance in thinking up *your* situation and *your* plot. As such, you could find them extremely valuable at times. But it would be far better to throw them away than to allow yourself to use them to constrain your own talent.

Chapter Seven

COLOURING CHARACTER

Certainly, in the very short form of short story, it is possible to tell a good tale using an interesting plot or theme and some well constructed characters who will act out the story for the reader. You will only have need (and only have sufficient words) to mention the furniture and scenery amidst which the action takes place. In our first story, CLEAN OUT OF CLUES, only the briefest mention was made of the premises in which Probend solved the crime. In THE CON, only enough information was given to set the scene as a sick-room. And these 'sets' were not given in the form of author's direct descriptions, but as areas in which the characters moved and spoke. Let us just recap with a sentence from early in THE CON.

> From where he lay in the bed he could see her rinse the glass, wipe it dry and put it with all of the other demned paraphernalia they kept out there for him.

That is not solely the author describing the scenery for the benefit of the reader. It is partly description but the use of the phrase *damned* paraphernalia suggests that we have almost caught the tetchy patient thinking aloud. We also *see* the nurse rinse a glass, wipe it dry and put it with all of the other paraphernalia. Finally, we read that this paraphernalia is something which 'they kept out there for him', which reveals that others, to some extent, are controlling his activities, albeit with his approval and at his expense. This information has been given to a very large extent by the actions and thoughts of the characters.

An unskilled writer may have handled it like this:—

Next to his bedroom, the bathroom contained all the requirements necessary for his medical care.

You will probably agree that this sentence is completely devoid of any human activity. It is sterile – colourless.

Which brings us to the next essential writing ability after characterisation. And that is the ability to introduce *colour* to the story over and above adequate characterisation.

We use the word colour quite deliberately. If we were to say atmosphere, scenery, setting or background, then we mean that we are adding *new factors* to the story. And, quite often, these new factors will be nothing more than padding.

Of course, it may be necessary to describe the elements, scenery, furniture, fittings and other gubbins in the story when these are *essential to the story*. If the murderer is going to bury his victim, we have to provide him with some earth to dig and a spade to dig it with. The point is, that these essentials should usually get no more words than they deserve – and that is next to nothing.

What we are talking about is colour. And what we mean by that is heightening up what is already there in the form of characterisation. Making it have more effect on the emotions and feelings of the reader. So, if the murderer is going to dig a grave, have him act it out with the props you provide.

He pushed the edge of the spade into the soil as he walked along the stone wall. He needed a soft spot that he could dig out deep and fast. The drizzle was coming down heavier now, and he wanted to get the last part over fast, then get back to Stepney and pick up his pay for the job.

The digging of the grave for the unfortunate victim has now become an extended revelation of the murderer's character. We have 'coloured' him, made him even more unlikable and callous by making the choice of spot in which to bury the victim as just part of the job, without a trace of remorse or guilt.

It is quite possible that you have not the slightest intention of committing any paper murders, but would prefer to write romances taking place in sunnier climes. Even here, you should present your scenery and coconut palms as part of colouring the words and actions of your characters.

What you must avoid, at all costs, is to write a travel brochure instead of your romance.

The Hotel del Posh stood overlooking the bay where the little fishing boats bobbed gently up and down against the old crumbling stone quay. The mid-day sun blazed across the silver plated water, sending the last of the old fishermen into the welcome shade for their siesta. Behind the hotel, the rocky hills strode up to the sky, their cloaks of fig trees and vines basking in the heat and making money for their owners as they dozed.

This is the kind of writing which soon has the average reader dozing. It is far, far better to key this kind of material to the thoughts, actions and words of your characters.

Mary dropped a coin into the ready hand of the porter as he placed her bags near the bed. 'Anything you want, senorina?' he asked.

'It's dark in here,' she said, walking toward a shuttered window.' And my sister says that the water in the bay is silver at this time of day.'

The porter grinned and shook his head. 'Best you not let the hot air in now, senorina. Best you be like the old fishermen down there and take your siesta. You want to go up in the hills, you go there when it not too hot.'

In this last version it is true that not so much detail of the scenery is given, but it is given by the two characters. It has given them colour. The bobbing boats and figs and olives may all be introduced in due course, if you wish — but do, please, introduce them in the course of your characters acting out the story. If the mid-day heat is so oppressive in this particular place, then you should use it to further the activities of the characters. Perhaps you could have Mary caught out under the broiling sun in a dramatic situation, or have it affect her behaviour or judgment in a way that will develop the story. What ever you do, use it as *colour* and not as simple description.

Chapter Eight

SETTING SCENES

So far, we have said that the writing of the short story and any kind of story depends for its effectiveness on the use of seemingly real characters which are well characterised. They should act out for the reader both the story and the feelings which the author wishes to arouse in his reader. We have also said colour should be added to the story by means of the characters moving about in the setting.

Having made these two points, we must now say that they cannot completely sustain the telling of the longer type of short story. It *is* necessary for the author to play the part of the storyteller to some degree. There are occasions when the characters cannot do all of the work themselves. But these occasions are far fewer than realised by the average beginning writer. The thing to remember is that there should be a balance between techniques. The characters should carry out the lion's share of the work, with the author setting the scene for them whenever it is essential. Please note that we did not say that the author sets the *scene*. He sets the scene *for them* – the characters. And, by now, you should be much better aware of the essential difference between these two activities. The author can set the scene for the *characters* – not for the *reader*.

Let us now take an example, so that you may read through it slowly and study how the author used all three of these techniques. The story can be classed under George Polti's Second Situation – Deliverance.

A seed for a silver rupee

The monk walked with measured steps down the stony path that led to the valley which cut through these grey rock hills, and promised water where a little vegetation sprang out of the yellow ground. Many years had passed since last he came by this way. There was a man and his wife and two small boys, he recalled. They honoured his orange robe by asking him to share what little food they had. They called the oldest boy by the name of Ram. The other's name he could not remember.

If they were still here they would surely make him just as welcome again, of that he could be certain, for these isolated farmers of poor soil were traditionally willing hosts to any traveller hungrier than themselves. They did not follow the teachings of Our Lord Buddha, nor any other religious calling that had a name, but instinctively gave freely of themselves to those who needed help and understanding.

He came to the dwelling of mud brick and saw that it was in good repair. The dry earth around was smooth from regular sweeping, and gave evidence that a caring woman's hand worked hard here. He stopped at the customary ten paces from the door and waited.

Soon she came out with a bowl of scraps to throw to the bantam hens which scratched in the gravel a short distance away. 'Forgive me for not knowing you were here, Holy One,' she said. 'Our humble house is honoured by your shadow.'

'And may peace be on all who live here,' he said in his quiet voice. 'It would please me to see again the man who built this house with his own hands.'

'Alas, both he and his woman are long dead. Now this house belongs to the eldest son, Ram. And I am the wife of Ram.' She pulled the edge of her simple sari slightly over her eyes, as she realised that her young tongue had run away by speaking of herself so soon. 'Can I give you some food and drink, Holy One?'

'Thank you, child – a little water. When you and your husband, and the children, have eaten tonight I will gladly accept what you do not need.'

'We have no children. There is only Ram and myself.'

'And is Ram here?'

'He will return this evening. Will you come inside and wait for him?'

'No. I must walk and meditate for a few more hours today. Tell Ram that I will return before the day is over.'

He drank from the chatti of cool water that she brought from the well and left her prowling after one of the hens. A little way from the house he climbed a mound of boulders and

44

sat looking over Ram's house and the ground that was cleared of rocks. A small stream ran close-by, rippling over pebbles only ankle-deep. Quite clearly, Ram was never short of water, for this was the driest part of the year. There was enough of this semi-fertile ground to feed a small village, that was sure. And yet there was so little planted. The quarter of maize would not provide many meals, and the beans even less. He closed his eyes and pictured how the view would be with mangoes, plantain and almond trees in full blossom. The empty vegetable patches would be in lush green leaf, and the sound of goat and duck would be heard over the buzz of the honey bee. He came down from where he sat and twisted his staff down into the earth, finding that there was no rock at seed depth. What kind of man had this Ram grown to be? There was certainly merit in keeping the land so orderly, but even the Lord Buddha would be dismayed at this failure.

He saw the young man hurrying towards him with a great load of dead branches for the fire stretched across his shoulders. His lips were dry, and the dust which coated his bare legs up to the knees gave fair indication that he was returning from a long distance.

'Peace be with you, young brother,' the monk said.

Under the burden he carried, Ram twisted his head to see who greeted him. 'And with you, Holy One,' he smiled. 'The house that you see is mine. But for as long as you are here it is also yours, and everything in it. You will, of course, honour me with a visit.'

'I will visit with you, Ram. Oh yes, I know your name. We met before when you were a child. You were quite talkative then.'

'I am a man now, Holy One,' Ram laughed. 'I will respect your right to silence. Come, you shall wash and eat, then rest on my best carpet.'

The monk ate the plain food slowly, taking less than Ram or his wife, and politely refusing one mouthful more. The young woman collected the bowls and took them to the stream for washing.

'You must excuse me now, Holy One,' Ram said. 'There is a little daylight left and I must tend to my crops.'

'Tomorrow will soon be here, young brother. And there will be much more daylight in which to tend them.'

'Ah, but I must leave early in the morning,' Ram said. 'And I shall not return until the same time as today.'

45

'And where shall you go tomorrow?'

'To visit my brother on the other side of the hill. His ground is full of stones and his crops will not grow unless he clears them all the day. It is too much work and I must give him help.'

'How long have you been helping him, young brother?'

'For three years,' Ram said. 'And it will be a long, long time before I can stop. You see, Holy One, I spend nearly half my day on the journey, so the work proceeds slowly.'

'Can you and your wife not stay with your brother and save the travelling time?'

Ram shrugged his shoulders resignedly. 'My father made me promise that I would stay with this land.'

'Then your brother should live here with you.'

'But he is married, Holy One. My father made him promise that if he ever took a wife, he would move to his own land, because two women under the same roof can cause a war in the home.'

'Then you could both tend your own land.'

'Yes, Holy One, that is what we hope to do one day. But our father also made us both promise that we would help each other in times of need. Are we foolish to keep these promises, Holy One?'

'No,' the monk said. 'But your father was unwise. You do not have children, Ram.'

Ram shook his head sadly. 'No. I will not bring children into the world that I cannot feed. And my brother says the same. Both of our wives are unhappy, Holy One. My brother and I are unhappy. But what can we do? If we were religious perhaps we could pray for a miracle.'

'One does not have to be religious to ask for help, Ram.'

'Could I ask for help, Holy One?' Ram asked in surprise.

The monk smiled benignly. 'I will help you, Ram. A miracle you shall have. Do you have any money?'

'I have one silver rupee, Holy One. My father gave it to me and made me promise that I would never spend it.'

'Then we must be sure that you never break your promise, Ram. This is what you must do. Three nights from now you must take your silver rupee to your brother's house. When they are asleep, you must enter the house. You will search the floor carefully until you find a seed, which you will place in your mouth. Then you will leave the rupee by your sleeping

46

brother's hand, and steal out of the house as quietly as you entered. This is what you must do.'

'But, Holy One!' Ram exclaimed. 'I shall have broken my promise to my father!'

'No,' the monk said firmly. 'For then a miracle will take place. With the seed in your mouth, you will return here to your home. Before the sun rises, you must plant that seed and water it. Four nights later, you must drop one of some seeds I shall give you on your floor and you must sleep with only pure thoughts in your head. In the morning you shall awake to find a silver rupee near to your hand.'

Ram rolled his eyes in terror. 'But this is magic, Holy One! If a terrible goblin should enter my house with the silver rupee in its claws, my heart would stop.'

'If you care for the seed you have planted, no goblin shall ever enter your house. Three nights later, you will take the silver rupee to your brother's house and repeat all these actions again.'

Ram leaned forward, his voice hushed with awe. 'For how long shall I receive these silver rupees, Holy One?'

The monk raised his shoulders vaguely. 'For as long as your brother needs your help. But, he added firmly. 'You must never visit your brother again in daylight, or the miracle will come to an end. Do you understand that?'

'Oh yes, Holy One,' Ram cried. 'There will be no need for me to go and help him each day, for with a silver rupee in his hand each week he will be able to feed his wife and himself and begin to make children.'

'And what about you, young brother?'

'I too can make children,' Ram laughed. 'I can have more time with my land. I can grow more food and help my brother as well. Will this really all come to pass, Holy One?'

'It will, Ram. But only if you raise whatever seeds you find on your brother's floor.' He took from within his robe a small sack of seeds and tipped them into Ram's hand. They were small and large, long and round, black and brown, and a sample of all the vegetables and fruit trees that he passed on his journeyings. 'These are the seeds you must leave on your floor to be changed into the rupees,' he said finally.

Ram salaamed and kissed the Holy One's feet many times before he could be persuaded to find his wife at the stream and tell her that they would begin to make children.

The monk stretched out full length on the threadbare carpet and smiled to himself. Soon Ram and his brother would be over their difficulties and no longer poor. The laughter of children would soon fill this silent place. If he returned in a few years, it should be at the season of fruit blossom. And he would make a special point of counting the goats and the ducks. He could almost taste the honey that Ram's wife would take from the hives.

He winced slightly at the lump which pushed against his ribs as he turned over to sleep. He put his hand beneath the orange robe and moved the other identical bag of seeds as he just gave to Ram.

Tomorrow, he would seek the hospitality of the younger brother. He would certainly wish to help Ram. With this bag of seeds, and the same story that had just been told, that single silver rupee would travel back and forth between the brothers, each time causing a seed to be planted for the future.

Miracles are so easy to understand when you know their secret.

Reprinted by permission of Fact & Fiction Agency.

Chapter Nine

STYLE

'What style shall I use in my writing?' 'Shall I use a Somerset Maugham style?' 'What writing styles do modern publishers prefer?' 'How can I improve my style?' These are the kind of questions which are often asked by new writers. They have probably heard the song, 'You gotta' have style', then shop around to find some.

Each writer will have his own individual way of speaking and writing, that is true. Some go in for short, direct sentences, whilst others use more words to present the same idea. Some use a simple vocabulary, and others give the impression that they have swallowed a very large dictionary.

But that is not what many new writers mean by 'style'. Their question is, in fact, a misquestion. And, as such, it can never be answered. This 'style' which puzzles them so much is not usually the style of the *author*, but the style in which the *story* is presented. If the author consistently writes stories in a particular category, then they will tend to be written with a similar flavour. The budding writer then assumes that this consistent way of presenting the stories is the author's 'style'. It is not.

There is one question which you can ask yourself and, once answered, you can then completely forget about this so-called author's style. Is your preference to present a story in the bold and direct manner? Or is it your wish to act on the reader's feelings in a more subtle manner? Adopt either method and your writing will stand on firm ground. Try to follow a middle course and your work will probably lack strength.

It is the story itself which determines the style in which it is best told. Our first example of the short-short story, CLEAN OUT OF

CLUES is really no more than a quick piece which has a surprise ending. The only 'style' involved in this piece is that the dialogue is spoken in the idiom of today. The same can almost be said of THE CON. It is taking place today, the dialogue is modern, and the story is told in very few words.

A SEED FOR A SILVER RUPEE has quite a different 'style'. It obviously takes place in India. But when? Today? Twenty-five years ago? A hundred years? There is a timeless quality about the venue and the situation. If you knew when the silver rupee was first used as currency, then you could date it to some degree. And there is a deliberate and somewhat dated manner in which the characters address each other. Is this because the story took place in earlier times? Is this how it would take place in India today? Or, has the author deliberately set about creating a feeling of 'foreignness'? Which ever it was, the author has certainly used a different 'style' for this story than the other two.

India and Buddha have been mentioned several times this far in this book, and we shall do so a few more times before we reach the end. All of the short stories used as examples were written by the same author. You should find it difficult to put your finger on an author 'style', although similar stories may seem to have a similarity in the telling.

Are we saying that all stories set in India and written by this author will all have the same flavour – the same 'style'? Not at all. Another story set in India, of a different period in time or of a different nature could have a 'style' which is quite different again. There may be minor similarities, but not many.

Let us see if you agree so far by asking you to study another Indian story by the same author.

Lord Dibdin's ants

Four days after leaving Jodhpur they came to the last water before they entered the starkness of the Thar Desert. For each of the Englishmen in the party there was an ox cart. Four ox carts, four English gentlemen, and Flaherty the servant of Lord Dibdin. The Indian porters set up the tents with unusual haste, for the white men were to continue alone into the desert the next morning, leaving the porters to laze in the shade until the return which was expected to be around one week later.

When the first tent was ready, Flaherty carried his master from the back of an ox cart and made him comfortable on a camp bed close to the table where the others would eat.

It was a simple meal of bully beef, ship's biscuits and fresh fruit, as would be their daily fare until they returned from their intrusion into the treacherous Thar. The only exception with this meal was the bottle of port which Flaherty opened and poured for them once the plates were cleared away.

Lord Dibdin raised his glass and sat as erect as he was able. 'Gentlemen,' he said. 'On this her birthday, I give you a toast to our gracious Queen Victoria, and long may she reign over us. Gentlemen, the Queen.'

'The Queen,' each of them replied, and drained his glass dry.

'Well, gentlemen,' Dibdin smiled. 'I told you that this would be a unique treasure hunt, and I promised that I would give you all the details once we reached the desert.' He waved his hand at the sandy waste which stretched before them. 'What would you like to know?'

The two younger men looked to Pelham to act as spokesman.

'The fact is, my lord, we know so little. And I might add that if we had not such a reputation as yours in which to place our confidence, it is hardly likely that we would have allowed ourselves to come this far on such scant information.'

'That is quite right, Pelham,' Dibdin said. 'And I sincerely thank you for that confidence. I must repeat what I told you at the very beginning, and that is that each of you could return from this adventure as an extremely wealthy man.'

'Is there really a king's ransom in gold, my lord?' the youngest man asked excitedly.

'If we could recover all of it, there would be just over five tons in weight.'

'Good Lord!' Pelham exclaimed. 'Why, that is over one ton for each of us. My lord, why didn't you tell us before that there was so much?'

'For the simple reason that I do not think it is worth the effort to gather any more than half of that quantity.'

'If you will pardon me for disagreeing with you,' Pelham said, 'I feel that any effort is worth while for an extra two and a half tons of gold. If it is a question of digging, we could easily take the native porters with us.'

Dibdin shook his head without the slightest hesitation. 'We dare not risk having any natives see what we do. And as for finding the gold, I must tell you that it is spread over an area

51

of some two square miles.' He held up his hand as they all rose to their feet. 'But, let me assure you, gentlemen – that at least a half of this treasure is located in a much smaller area. With my plan of action, we should be able to recover it and be away from the damned spot within a matter of days.'

'But what form does the gold take?' Pelham asked. 'Is it jewellery? Coins? Religious objects? Yes, it must be religious objects, for you fear upsetting the natives.'

'No, it is none of these things. It is fine gold dust. And be assured that this is the truth, for I have seen it with my own eyes. Open bags of gold dust which almost blinded me with their reflection of the light from the sun.'

'They are, of course, buried in a secret place,' Pelham said.

'I fear not,' Dibdin sighed. 'The gold will now be spread across the ground, quite thoroughly mixed with the desert sand.'

'Then our task is quite hopeless.'

'Not at all,' Dibdin laughed. 'Please allow me more credit than that, Pelham. We shall need help, of course. But I trust I have found a way to turn our deadliest enemy into a most willing worker on our behalf.'

The two young men looked at each other uncomfortably.

'Let me give you the full story,' Dibdin said. 'Many years ago I found myself lost in the desert where we shall go to-morrow. Mercifully, I had a fair horse and a little food and water. Imagine yourselves, gentlemen, out on thousands of square miles of sand, where the view in any direction is exactly the same as any other. You will appreciate my relief when I eventually saw a stone pillar on the horizon.'

'Were you able to identify it, my lord?' one of the young men asked.

'Indeed, yes. It was an inscribed Asoka monument. An early Asian ruler, you know. But, as soon as I arrived at it, I knew which direction I must take to arrive where we are now. But, I must tell you, gentlemen, I found more there than just the pillar.'

'The gold?' Pelham asked eagerly.

'I found the gold. I also found the skeletons of men and animals. It was the remains of a caravan, gentlemen. I did what I could in the form of a Christian burial, of course.'

'But the gold!' Pelham repeated.

'Ah, yes. There it was in many piles of damaged cloth sacks. The winds will certainly have spread it around by now.

52

But I have subsequently carried out experiments, gentlemen. And you may rest assured that gold dust, being heavy, does not travel far in the strongest of gales. Most of it will surely be close to Asoka's pillar.'

'You said that this took place many years ago, my lord,' said one of the young men.

'Yes, many years.'

'Then couldn't you have returned to recover the gold long before now?'

'No,' Dibdin said emphatically. 'You see, I could hardly believe my good fortune. I knew that I could be out of the desert within a very short time, so I decided to share my remaining food and water with the horse, and let us get a decent rest through the night which we both badly needed.'

'Then what went wrong,' Pelham asked.

Lord Dibdin's face creased in a deep frown. 'Just as dawn broke, I was awakened by the screams of my horse. I scrambled to my feet and could hardly believe my eyes. The horse was in agony, dripping blood from his mane to his tail, and covered in a thick blanket of ants that were eating him alive.'

The young men looked at each other anxiously.

'And what is more,' Dibdin continued. 'The whole of the desert sand was covered with them for a half mile in all directions. They were on my body, building up in great masses on my lower legs. I did the only thing I could, gentlemen — I shot my horse and ran in this direction as fast as my legs would carry me. I was found several days later, but septicaemia had taken a strong hold on my legs and they were both amputated, as you can see.'

Pelham fiddled with his empty glass, and there was not the usual force in his voice. 'It is quite possible that these ants still exist near the stone monument.'

'You may depend on it,' Dibdin smiled. 'And I can tell you that this is the same time of the year when I first met them. They will be quite hungry, gentlemen, indeed they should be ravenous.'

'Gold, or no gold,' Pelham growled, 'I have no fancy for having the flesh picked from my bones.'

'And nor shall you, my dear Pelham. You have my assurance that the ants will be far too busy collecting the gold for us.'

'Collecting the gold!' Pelham exclaimed. 'Oh, but this is an impossibility!'

53

'Not at all. You see, some years ago I came into possession of some old Indian texts which I found as enlightening as they were fascinating. We look at our world, gentlemen, and we claim that we are making progress. But, that is not so. We have, in fact, lost many of our natural abilities. We are not nearly as knowledgable as once we were. Many of our capabilities have gone so completely as to make one wonder if it has all been achieved with some deliberate intent.' He looked around at their faces, blank with bewilderment. 'But, more to the point, gentlemen, I discovered how it is possible to train ants to separate out grains of gold from grains of sand, and bring them to us as surely as a bird-dog retrieves his master's catch.'

Pelham shook his head in disagreement with the proposal. 'You said that we should only be there for a few days, my lord. It would take the ants all of that time to gather the gold, if that is possible. There would be no time in which they could be trained.'

'But they already are, Pelham,' Dibdin said. He turned to his servant. 'Bring me one case, Flaherty,' he called.

Flaherty took one of the flat cases from a cart and placed it on the ground near to where the men were sitting. He removed the lid and revealed a glass cover beneath which a thousand or more yellow ants scurried and wheeled in search of an exit. Dibdin took a small pouch from his waistcoat pocket and tossed it to Pelham. 'There is some gold dust,' he said. 'Take a small pinch and scatter it on the ground, if you please.'

Pelham sprinkled the glittering powder onto the dusty ground at his feet. Then, with a defiant glance at Dibdin, scuffed it criss-cross with the heel of his boot so that most of it could no longer be seen.

Dibdin smiled broadly. 'Excellent, my dear Pelham. Now, if you will just remove the glass cover from my little pupils.'

Pelham unlatched the grips which held down the glass and hesitated.

'Oh, come now!' Dibdin chuckled. 'There are certainly not enough of them in that box to strip you down to your bones.'

Pelham lifted the glass sheet, turned it over on the ground and leapt a few feet away. The ants came out of the box like milk boiling over in a pan. They circled around scenting and fanning out like the emission of a live catherine wheel. They came closer to where the gold dust lay, passing it in a widening stream, until a stray scout dashed out alone and came full halt at a speck of the precious metal. It froze for a full three seconds, then dashed full pelt into the racing procession, bumping, prodding and touching, until it was surrounded by a thick crowd of fellow hunters. Another three seconds passed as the message was relayed from the centre to the fringe, and they moved as a packed battalion to where Pelham had dropped their prize. Each of them snatched a speck of gold and returned to the box from which they had been released, dropping its burden inside and returning to find more. Soon the ground was picked clean, with the gold piled in a neat heap and the ants again moving around hectically inside the box. The men watched the spectacle in complete silence.

'Give them their pay, Flaherty,' Dibdin said.

From a jar that he took from one of the carts, Flaherty scooped out a small dob of honey and placed it inside the box. He tipped the gold back into his master's pouch, covered the scrabbling ants and took them away.

'Well, gentlemen?' Dibdin asked.

'It is nothing short of a miracle, my lord. As you say, the gold will be recovered. But I have two doubts. How long will it take them to collect two and a half tons? And will the wild ants of the desert leave us in peace?'

'We have with us a total of one hundred boxes such as you have just seen, my dear Pelham. And you will agree that they are extremely fast workers. But there is something else I have not told you. A few years ago Flaherty and myself came here and selected some of these wild ants. From those few, I have bred and rebred and trained until I have a strain which has only two purposes in life, the collecting of gold and an overwhelming desire for honey. I told you that my old Indian texts are full of fascinating information. Part of them deal with the subject of communication. Have you any idea how you communicate with an ant, Pelham?'

'No, my lord, I confess that I have no idea at all.'

'It is so simple,' Dibdin said. 'You have another ant do it for you. And that is the answer to your fear concerning the wild ants we shall surely meet. In fact, we must be quite sure that we do meet. Our insects will lead the others to do our bidding. We shall have untold millions of them recovering our treasure. May I assume that this plan is to your satisfaction, gentlemen?'

It was to their complete satisfaction, and they would have discussed it through the night had not Dibdin reminded them of their early start the following day.

They left the native porters behind just as the first shaft of sunlight painted a path into the Thar Desert, and arrived at the Asoka column in the full heat of noon. Soon the tents were erected, giving some welcome shade, and a kettle of water boiled its readiness for making tea. The meal was soon over, for food at this moment was nothing more than something to fill their bellies until their task was completed.

'Shall we make a start and release the ants now?' Pelham asked.

'Not today,' Dibdin said. 'In the morning we shall open a few boxes to test that we do not have any unsuspected problems. If all goes well, then each of you and Flaherty will take a cart off in a different direction, leaving me here to feed our little group of workers. You will each travel for five hours, opening sufficient cases of ants at regular intervals along the way, so that you will have finished and be able to return at the end of that five hours. If you leave at dawn, you should be back here at sunset.'

'But shall we be safe out there?' Pelham asked.

'You will be if you have plenty of honey,' Dibdin insisted. 'Take all of it with you, making sure that I have a large pot to reward my own little group. Have no worries, gentlemen. Tomorrow we shall just be preparing the ground. The day after, our own workers will be returning with their pupils, and we shall be able to sit here and watch ourselves becoming wealthy.'

At first light the following day, they released a few boxes of ants close to Dibdin's camp bed. As he predicted, they began gathering gold immediately and piled it on the glass sheets near to him. After a few drops of the sweet syrup, they again journeyed out, gradually timing their circuit until they moved back and forth in a continual stream.

Dibdin took a second pot of honey from Flaherty and stood it with the other on the bed beside him. 'Very well, gentlemen,' he said. 'Off you go. I look forward to seeing you again at sundown.'

The ox carts creaked their way across the hard packed sand, fanning out into a semi-circle that would eventually be twenty miles across. Flaherty's cart was the first to stop. Shading his eyes against the early morning glare, Dibdin watched the servant bending to the ground as he shook out a box of ants to search for recruits. Pelham was the next, and then the younger of the two other men. Soon they were out of sight, and he gave his attention to the doling out of honey, a single drip at a time as the ants filed over the edges of the boxes for their reward.

By ten o'clock the reflected heat from the ground began to shimmer and the sharpness of the horizon became lost to him in liquid waves of movement. By now the ox carts would be ten miles or more out on their journeys, with more than a quarter of their tiny passengers set free.

Three times he shook tiny mountains of gold dust into a canvas sack. He rubbed his arm against the cramp which came from leaning over the edge of his cot and dripping steady drops of honey into the teeming boxes.

An hour later he jerked himself awake from the monotonous doze into which he had fallen and found that the collection of dust had almost come to a halt, with the ants crowding their boxes in search of the sweet syrup. He quickly recharged their empty feeding dishes and watched as they licked them clean. Once again they filed out to find dust. When most of them were out, he noticed a different kind of activity within one of the boxes.

A dozen or so were milling around in an untidy group. Around them three smaller ants circled quickly like sheepdogs. He peered closer. Those being so effectively shepherded were not his own ants, for they were larger and of a darker yellow. Then, they came over the side of the box in a flock and raced towards the shadow of Asoka's pillar, where no searching had yet begun.

Dibdin smiled with satisfaction. The recruiting had already started. No need to wait until tomorrow for them; they had already started to trickle in. He imagined to himself the impression this success would have on the other men when they returned at sundown.

He opened the second pot of honey just after noon, and snatched a few mouthfuls of food and water between his steady serving of the ants. He looked at his watch and saw that he had more than enough honey to last until the sun set and they rested from their labours.

By one o'clock, thin yellow trails like Demerara sugar were ranging in from all directions towards him, each of them with its own small attachment of tiny marshals heading off the

57

strays and herding them back into the working columns.

Now the gold dust was coming to him at four times the speed, with two canvas sacks completely full and another half way to the top. The honey was being depleted much faster as well, and he began to eke it out with small additions of his drinking water. He looked again at the surrounding desert, now alive for as far as he could see with wave after wave of sparkling yellow bands.

At two o'clock precisely, he shook the last of the slightly sweetened water out of the jar and threw it to one side. If his legs were still complete, he could have walked within a diameter of twenty feet without the taking of life. From that point on, they swarmed an inch thick on the ground, with as many again spread out behind and forcing their way in.

His own ants held a guard line between the wild ones and himself, pressing back any significant bulges towards him.

He looked at his watch again. Another four hours would pass before his companions returned with any lifesaving supplies of honey. He would have to rely until then on his own ants holding off the others.

He smiled grimly as he recalled another two of the axioms concerning communication that were mentioned in his old Indian texts. Communication is a two-way affair. And you have to be prepared, if only occasionally, to let him impress his own ideas on you.

His own ants had never had the opportunity to taste live meat. He hoped for all he was worth that they would resist any attempt to talk them into it.

Reprinted by permission of Fact & Fiction Agency

In the author's opinion, the best period for the action of this story was in Victorian times. It was necessary for there to be a lack of modern technology – no artificial limbs for Lord Dibdin, for instance. No powered vehicles or radio.

So the Victorian period was chosen, which decided the social divisions of the characters and their style of conversation. Now, if the characters are going to use formal and dated conversation, the narrative of the story cannot be too dissimilar. In fact, the whole of the writing is dated to some small degree. It moves at a much slower pace than CLEAN OUT OF CLUES or THE CON, but moves at a faster pace than A SEED FOR A SILVER RUPEE. Ideally, the story should have started with some immediate action on the part of the characters, but there was some advance information that the reader would need. The author decided to take the plunge and present this 'flashback' immediately and as quickly as possible. You can get away with it most of the time with this type of story, but the general rule is to start with character action if it is at all possible.

Each of the examples given in this book has its own 'style'.

So, in future, do not overly concern yourself too much with adopting a 'style'. Concern yourself with what techniques you use for presenting a particular kind of story. If you look to the writings of others for study of the short story form, look for the author's technique. And the best techniques of all are the ones which don't jump out of the page at you.

Chapter Ten

BEGINNINGS

'Where shall I begin my story?' That is the question of every writer of fiction, be he a novice or a household name. For the beginning of a story is the most important part of all. Every story also has a middle and an end which also carry their own measure of importance for the overall effect which the author is trying to achieve. But the beginning bears the main load. Not only does it have to hold the reader's interest, but it has to create that interest in the first place.

Each author tends to develop his own technique in story beginnings. One will start with a 'day that is different'. Another will choose a 'moment of change'. And yet another decides on 'a decision must be made'. All of these are quite valid and, well written, will appeal to the reader's inherent curiosity.

But the better kind of beginning is the one which seems to be the most reasonable one for *that* story. Now this may seem to be oversimplifying the problem and hardly answers the question of 'where shall I begin my story?'.

More often than not, we do not truly know our story to its fullest degree until we have written it. So how can we write a beginning that is best suited to it until we know what the story *is*? The answer is really quite simple. You don't write the beginning until you have written the story in full.

What you do is to write *any kind* of a beginning which will get you off to a start. It doesn't even have to be a good beginning, because you will eventually come back to it and either scrap or rewrite it. It is as simple as that!

One of the finest exercises for the new writer is to study other authors' beginnings. So let us examine a few here. We shall use some examples of authors long dead.

Dr. Manette's MS – Charles Dickens

I, Alexandre Manette, unfortunate physician, native of Beauvais, and afterwards resident of Paris, write this melancholy paper in my doleful cell in the Bastille, during the last month of the year 1767.

In one sense, this is a wonderful example of how not to write a modern-day beginning. It is the kind of beginning which is often used by novice writers. It is both 'dated' and intended to draw pity to the story-telling character. It is the kind of beginning to be avoided at all costs. But it does pack a considerable amount of information into only thirty-two words. And what is more, that information conjures up an emotionally slanted picture of this man's sorry plight.

Malachi's Cove – Anthony Trollope

On the northern coast of Cornwall, between Tintagel and Bossiney, down on the very margin of the sea, there lived not long since an old man who got his living by saving seaweed from the waves, and selling it for manure.

Once again, this is 'dated', but it moves straight into the story by giving us a quick identification of the character. Trollope lived between 1815–1882. Most of his contemporary authors had very long-winded beginnings. Trollope was not one of them, but preferred to move straight into his stories without a dignified preamble. It was a relatively new device for his time, but now it is absolutely essential.

A Dreudful Bell – Leopold Lewis

It was one of those large and important hotels that seem to swoop down and take possession of little villages.

Only twenty words here, yet a surprisingly sharp combination of atmosphere, setting and preparation for what is to follow considering that it was written before 1890.

My Fare – George Manville Fenn

Don't you make a mistake now, and think I'm not a working man, because I am.

This a story, told in the first person singular, by a driver of a horse and cab. He is a somewhat prickly character, and these first few words establish that fact very quickly.

An Alpine Divorce – Robert Barr

In some natures there are no half-tones; nothing but raw primary colours. John Bodman was a man who was always at one extreme or the other. This would probably have mattered little had he not married a wife whose nature was an exact duplicate of his own.

Once again, not the kind of beginning which is favoured today, but at least making the reader aware that he can expect trouble ahead.

The King is Dead, Long Live The King – Mary Coleridge

It was not very quiet in the room where the king lay dying.

This story beginning was written eighty years ago. Many modern authors would be hard put to present such a definite picture in so few words.

The Hero of Waterloo – Bernard Capes

Colonel Manton put up his rod and demanded to be put ashore. It had been his first experience of coarse fishing on the river and it had not proved to his taste.

The author does not tell the reader that Colonel Manton is in a foul temper, he lets the Colonel act it out.

Inside-out – Laurence Housman

Bunder-Runder was in jail. He was there for having talked too much, for saying things which the owners of the jail did not at all like, and which those who did not own the jail liked only too well.

There are three implied questions to the reader here. What has Bunder-Runder been saying? Who owns the jail? And who are these other people who do not own the jail?

The King of the Baboons – Perceval Gibbon

The old yellow-fanged dog-baboon that was chained to a post in the yard had a dangerous trick of throwing stones.

Once more a very distinct picture which immediately moves into the story.

Mr. Tolman – Frank R. Stockton

Mr. Tolman was a gentleman whose apparent age was of a varying character.

This story was also written over eighty years ago. The author was American, which may account for the directness of the beginning.

The Idyll of Red Gulch – Francis Bret Harte

Sandy was very drunk. He was lying under an azalea-bush, in pretty much the same attitude in which he had fallen some hours before.

Once more – every picture tells a story.

My Favourite Murder – Ambrose Bierce

Having murdered my mother under circumstances of singular atrocity, I was arrested and put upon trial, which lasted seven years.

Well, he didn't waste any time in telling us about it, did he?

The Trimmed Lamp – O. Henry

Of course there are two sides to the question. Let us look at the other.

The Last Leaf – O. Henry

In a little district west of Washington Square the streets have run crazy and broken themselves into small strips called 'places'.

The Belled Buzzard – Irvin S. Cobb

There was a swamp known as Little Niggerwool, to distinguish it from Big Niggerwool, which lay across the river.

When did you write your mother last? – Addison Lewis

Collins was a bum. He roamed about the country on foot or abaft the rods of wind-jamming freight cars, summer and winter, a restless spirit whose sole desire was to get food enough to keep him alive and beer as often as possible.

This chapter concerns the beginnings of stories. The purpose of the beginning is to establish what is going to be developed in the middle and resolved in the ending. So, the examples given above are not complete beginnings, but the first sentence or so of the stories. Even so, you will apreciate that they have achieved that other purpose of the beginning, and that is to take hold of the reader's interest.

As we said earlier, the beginning of a story is best written after the story is completed. You just cannot spend enough effort on getting it just right. Writing the effective beginning is purely a matter of technique, and this you can develop in yourself by studying how the other fellow did it.

The examples given here are still dated, even if they are good. You should now take every opportunity to collect some modern examples of your own. And, even if you do not have a story to write at the moment – write some intriguing beginnings. You may even develop some story ideas from them.

Chapter Eleven

RADIO SHORT STORY

So far we have been discussing the short and the short-short story which is written for publication in print. There is another kind of story, which is written to be read for a listener – and this is usually the radio, although TV uses work such as this from time to time.

This kind of story requires a somewhat different technique from that which is going to appear on the printed page. The story for the spoken voice is not just a story which happens to be read aloud, but is particularly tailor-made for the job. Failing to understand the importance between the two is the reason why many short story writers never hear their work broadcast. The only other mistake which can be made is in writing the wrong *type* of story for radio. Writing for the spoken voice is quite easy to learn, but when it comes to writing a suitable *type* of story, some writers just never seem to learn.

For instance, animal stories are hardly ever taken for adult listening. Quite often for children, but never for adults. And yet these animal stories are the ones that are most often offered to broadcasting stations. 'My cat, Diddles.' 'Ozzie the Goldfish.' 'How Billie Budgie Won Through.'

So, what kind of story is suitable for radio? Before that question can be answered, you have to consider who is likely to listen to it. A car mechanic could be listening to his transistor. A patient in hospital could be listening with the aid of earphones – if he is fortunate enough to have the rare set which works. Soldiers, and sailors at sea quite often listen in to radio. And then there are the millions and millions of other people from convicts to film stars, and hairdressers to pensioners. This is the potential of the radio audience and the short story producer has the difficult task of finding something which appeals to almost everyone.

This may seem to be quite impossible, but it can be done to a great extent by eliminating certain *categories* of fiction. Take crime stories, for instance. You could say that by not broadcasting crime stories, the producer does not cater for those who prefer crime stories. That may be perfectly true but, at the same time, he has not caused those listeners who cannot bear crime stories at any price to switch off.

It is quite evident that if he does not use anything which causes people to switch off, then he has kept them listening in. And that is the whole basis of selecting short stories for radio.

For the general purpose short story programme, it is 'No' to crime, detection, pure romance, ghost stories, fantasy and horror. It is a definite 'No' to pet and animal stories which would cause he-men and with-it teenagers to wilt. It is 'No' in capital letters to anything scarey or in dubious taste.

These are the kind of stories which are not suitable. This means that suitable stories are of a more general character. And, if you listen in regularly, you will find this to be the case.

You will also find that these stories tend to take the middle ground between high comedy and heavy drama. This does not mean that they are of a neutral character, but contain the elements of humour and drama to a lighter degree.

When you have decided what your story is to be, you have to decide on its length. For a fifteen-minute story this would be 2,150 words, allowing just a little more for trimming to exact time in the studio.

Your story will probably be read by a professional actor or actress. Before you start writing, you must decide which of these it is to be, because that will determine how the story will be told.

Should it be a young reader — or of more mature years? Well-spoken or of a rougher tongue? Then you must decide on the nationality or dialect. All important factors to be decided before you can put a word to paper — because your story is going to be *acted*. You are going to write a part for an actor which happens to be a short story.

As a professional, your reader will relish the opportunity to have one or two 'parts' to play in your story. This is character acting within the overall piece.

Let us suppose that you write your story to be told by a middle-aged middle-class lady, and she is telling us about a 'war' which takes place between her mother and the District Nurse. For the main part of the story, the actress will be just what you need her to be – a middle-aged, middle-class lady. When she speaks as Grannie, her voice will perhaps drop and become gravelly – and perhaps waspish.

In a *written* story you could have her say: 'Where have you been? I've been on my own for hours!' Grannie said waspishly. For a written story, that would be fine. But, your actress will *say* these words waspishly. You only write down – she said. It is worth spending a moment or so to get that clear before moving on.

You would want the District Nurse to be as different as possible to the middle-aged lady and her mother – but well within the range of the actress's capabilities. You could arrange for her to be in her early thirties and Irish born. You do not put this in your manuscript as stage-directions, but the same as you would in any short story. Your middle-aged lady could say;

> Within the next few minutes, Nurse Rooney would arrive, bringing with her Grannie's medicine, her young enthusiasm and more than a touch of Irish Blarney. Any one of which were guaranteed to bring Grannie's guns up into firing position.

So, your short story has, in fact, now become something of a playlet – with three spoken voices – all coming from the one actress reader.

But what if your story does not have a District Nurse? Your third character is Grandad. How can the reader speak with her own voice, Grannie's Voice, and the male voice of an elderly man? Well, she doesn't need to – because you paraphrase what Grandad says so that we don't actually hear him.

Something like this:

> Grannie stared at me closely as I forced down the second slice of fruit cake. 'You're too thin, girl,' she said. 'If you don't put on some more weight, you'll sicken for something!' She turned sharply towards Grandad and, almost as a challenge, said – 'She'll sicken for something, won't she?'
> Grandad rattled his newspaper and buried his head deeper with a mumbled word. He agreed with her up to a point, but this was no battle he was going to volunteer into.

We have all that we need of Grandad's response, but the actress did not need to play his part.

The writing of the radio short story is covered in detail in the

67

companion to this book, WRITING FOR RADIO & TV by the same author. We repeat here again what was said in that book — whenever you write a story which is to be read aloud, you get a better short story. A spoken story *has* to be conversational and thereby more intimate than a story which has a 'literary' flavour. Of course, there will be occasions when you use a literary style. There will be times, particularly in a novel, when you wish a character to reveal himself in poetic or beautiful prose. But it will rarely be in the short story.

The best attitude you can take when writing a short story is to imagine that you are chatting to *one* friend. This attitude becomes absolutely essential if your story is intended to be warm or humorous.

Which brings us back to humour again.

There is always a market for humour — if it is well written. The easiest type of humorous short story to write is in the first person singular viewpoint. That is, it is the author speaking directly to the reader. It becomes easier if the author adopts a 'character' for himself.

Earlier in this book|we took the example of THE BIG TOE. This is a short story. It has a plot, and it has characters, although we do not come immediately face-to-face with them. We can imagine that the teller of the story is a simple kind of soul, and is not quite aware of the fact that what he says is amusing to some people. He is the eternal innocent.

Humour tends to have rules all of its own. You can do anything you wish in order to amuse. You may even construct the piece so that it nearly, but not quite, follows the structure of an article or essay.

Let us look at an example which has been broadcast in several countries. Once again, it is told by the author to the reader/listener, and the author assumes again the role of the eternal innocent. It falls between the forms of short-short story and the humorous article.

The Habit

(To be read by a middle-aged 'vicar' type)

Some people have simply awful habits. Like kissing the neighbour's wife. But not me. She is nearly seven foot tall, anyway. And I am certainly not going to take up pole vaulting for one brief moment of madness.

No, I decided against that long ago. I am like that — honest,

68

upright – and very much a coward.

There are all kinds of things that I could give up doing. But I don't have to – because I don't do them anyway.

I make a definite rule to only indulge myself in those things which are not habit-forming. Like visiting Russia, kissing babies and eating at Monty's cafe. Many things I will not permit myself to do, because one day I know I would want to stop. I find that an excellent habit to adopt.

And I am not prepared to waste my time on things which are not worth starting.

Oh yes, I can give up most things I do do – or may do. But I have one quite uncontrollable habit. Silly, silly me – I blush with shame. But, that's enough of that as the hen said to the ostrich.

I cannot stop myself from going to a certain shop. It sells sweets, tobacco, newspapers, and other things which are not very good for you. It is an unbelievably horrid shop. Untidy, smelly. Opens late. Closes early. And it goes off to lunch for half the day. Quite a cosmic disaster in its own small way.

And I just cannot stay away. Like gravity, I seem to be magnetized towards it.

It isn't as if I had a particular fondness for the hovel. In fact it depresses me, and my nervous rash flares up like a sunspot every time I go there. And it really isn't convenient for me to get to. I have to catch two buses. Not at the same time, I should add. One after the other.

A soul-destroying journey. Almost as bad as visiting Russia. It just goes to show how much of a grip it has on me.

The married couple who own it are not at all pleasant. You probably wouldn't like them. They certainly wouldn't like you.

I have never yet been in there without him asking me if I had the right change. And feeling like a criminal if I said no. These days I take two whole pockets of coins to be on the safe side.

And oft-times he's given me my gardening magazine minus the free gift. The number of sweet pea seeds and pruning guides I've been deprived of must be quite phenomenal.

He's a fellow who takes things personally, and he has favourites. Like taking my free gifts and giving them to his relatives. It certainly wouldn't be to other customers – because they don't like customers. And that's certainly all right with us customers, because we are not madly in love with those two,

69

either.

And the wife! Oh dear, oh dear! Nobody deserves to be married to her. Not even him. Talk about a booming voice. She can't even whisper without things falling off the shelves.

At first, I thought she was deaf. You know how you do.

She was awfully rude. Even tried to pick up the counter and shake it at me. I am sure she would have become quite physical if her husband had not had the presence of mind to heave me out through the door.

And still I go there. In spite of always feeling unwelcome. You see, you have to behave yourself. You really do. There is a notice on the door saying 'no smoking no dogs'. Which I consider to be both bad English and an insult to one's intelligence. You may be able to smoke a kipper. But a dog? Never!!!!

Underneath that is 'no ice creams, lollies, prams and chips to be brought onto these premises.'

They sell birthday cards, but heaven help you if you touch one. I do believe that if a fly should settle on a wish-you-were-here, they would swat it with a what-you-damage-you-pay-for notice.

It goes without saying that shop-lifters will be prosecuted. Which, at least, consoles the shop-lifters with the thought that the safety of police protection is not too far away.

And you must close the door behind you. That is quite obligatory. Many an offender has been hauled back to the scene of the crime for that offence.

And still I go there. It really is an awful habit, I know. I should make the difficult effort to break it.

If only I could find the courage, I should march boldly in there with an unsmoked dog sitting in a pram. Chomping away extrovertly on my ice lolly and chips, and shouting wildly whilst I handled the cards.

I should then take something without paying – such as my sweet pea seeds and pruning guides, and depart the place for ever – leaving the door wide open behind me.

That's what I should do.

But, as I have already said – I am not given to starting what I may wish to stop one day. That is really not the sort of habit that I would care to have.

I shall just have to put up with it – that's all!

Reprinted by permission of Fact & Fiction Agency.

Chapter Twelve

ORCHESTRATION

So far we have strongly pressed the point that the strength of a short story depends on the construction of the story characters and how the reader sees them behave. We now come to another aspect of characterisation, and that is orchestration. We use the term orchestration in exactly the same way that it is used in the field of music, and that is as a score or arrangement for a piece of music. In our case it is the arrangement of a number of characters for a short piece of fiction.

If there is one major error that a beginning writer is going to make in a short story, it is by having too many characters. There are several good reasons for having a minimum of characters. Probably the most important is the shortness of story time in which the reader has to get to know them. In a book which concerns Joe Bloggs, you have both the room and the story time with which to introduce Joe's family, friends, neighbours, employers and enemies. Which is just fine if you wish to present Joe as a full-blown character with a realistic social background and as a three-dimensional figure.

But, with the short story, you quite intentionally draw at most a two-dimensional character. And in the short-short story, a one-dimensional character. You only paint in the most necessary of characteristics. So, you have to learn to orchestrate each individual character so that he or she has a balanced personality – the balance being the ideal one for presenting the particular story.

When you add one or more characters, orchestration becomes even more important. They must not only be different from each other, but the reader must *see* that they are different. This does not mean that one must be a goody and the other a baddy, or one must be young and the other old. It is best exampled by a piece of music which has been orchestrated for two pianos. A duet. The pianists do not play the same notes at the same time, neither do they play two different pieces. Just imagine one playing *Greensleeves*, and the other *Skaters Waltz!* No doubt a clever arranger could make some kind of sense of it. But it would still be something of a dog's dinner.

In the great majority of stories you will need a main character, and you must keep firmly in mind that this character is going to draw most of the reader's interest. He is the spokesman of the story or, in musical terms, the player who will play the main theme of the piece. If it is at all possible, you will manage with only one more character with which to tell the story. This second character will also be as real as you can make him in the limited number of words that are available to you, but he should always take the part of the second fiddle and, by and large, every word that he says or action that he takes should supplement the main character or be essential to the story.

In a book length story, our principal character, Joe Bloggs, could have a number of adversaries. Bill could be after his girl friend, Tom could be after his job, Dick has wrecked his car and Harry owes him money and refuses to pay up. In a book length story, there is probably enough room and time for Joe to be seen suffering from the actions of all these terrible people. In the short story there is not. There is only enough room for one villain. What is more, this villain must get secondary treatment to Joe in the story.

As far as the shortness of a short story will allow, you must also introduce your characters one at a time, so that the reader is able to grasp who is doing what. This is often more easier said than done, but it is most important and the author has to make some reasonable attempt to make it easy on the reader. Where ever possible, the story should start with the main character *in action*.

It is often said that the main character should be of the hero variety. One that the reader can identify with. This is all very well when the main character *is* a hero. But suppose that he is a villain? How do you make him likeable? Quite obviously you cannot always do this and remain credible with the reader. What you can do instead is to make him *interesting*. Interest alone can work marvels in this instance. If you visit the zoo, you will see some pretty unlikeable specimens; nothing which you could call a hero or want to identify with. But just let one of these creatures manifest its characteristics boldly, and it will soon hold your *interest*.

You will probably have your real live public figure that you love to hate. Why do you bother to hate him or her? Why can't you just turn your back and look the other way? The reason probably is, like it or not, that you find this figure interesting. You may say that this person is always being thrust before you by the media, but you still do not shrug him or her off as being uninteresting. You could almost say that anyone or anything presented to you effectively will capture your interest, even if only for a fleeting moment. It is this human response which the short story writer must play on. If you want your reader to show interest in anything or anyone – *make it interesting*. Advertising campaigns do it all the time. All detergent powders come from virtually the same source. Renamed as washing powders and given appealing names, slogans, packaging and characteristics, this basic material assumes a new quality. It becomes interesting.

Let us study an example of this making a villain interesting. We shall go back to a short short story, which limits the number of words available to us. The main character is a villain by the name of Jack Cox. Virtually every word in the story is designed to tell the story itself, to build Jack Cox into as many dimensions as possible, and to colour him. In other words, to make him interesting. There is no attempt to make him likeable.

Nothing to say

'When you have given the police your statement and signed it, you will say no more,' said Grimsby.

'As you never fail to remind me,' I said.

The solicitor carried on speaking as if he hadn't heard me. 'If they ask you any more questions, you will tell them that you have nothing further to say for the moment.'

'And if the worst comes to the worst,' I reminded him, 'you will fix it up that I get out on bail.'

'As we planned a few weeks ago,' he agreed. 'Rest assured that I will have you out in time to buy me an expensive lunch.'

I hadn't had a bite for 24 hours, and by now I should have been starving. But there are two things which can kill my appetite – excitement and bad company.

I was excited all right! With nearly 50 thousand pounds in untraceable notes safely hidden away, who wouldn't be? And all it had taken was a few hours hard and tricky work the night before.

As for bad company. All of Grimsby's legal diplomas, his made-to-order shoes *and* the Daimler we were riding in, couldn't have made him look any different to me than he was — a greedy and crooked lawyer.

Oh! He has his uses all right — if you don't mind paying for them. The fee he was charging me this time must have been as much as the Prime Minister makes in a year.

And all because I am a specialist.

Every time this particular brand of safe was picked, the police would ask me to call and account for my movements. Grimsby would come along and hold my hand. A cast-iron alibi always proved that I was somewhere else at the time. Grimsby could arrange proof that you were in outer space — *if* you paid him enough.

On six different occasions Detective Inspector Probend had questioned me, and the last time he made it pretty clear that I only just made it by the skin of my teeth.

It seems that an old lady caught a glimpse of my face as I was squeezing through a small window. The next day she died from natural causes. I had nothing to do with it, so help me, as I don't hold with violence. Nor did Grimsby, because he didn't charge me for it.

But it was a near thing for all that, and I soaked up some of Grimsby's confidence as he swung the car into a space clearly marked 'Reserved for Senior Officers.'

'You can rest your cheque book on that,' he said, sliding his shark-skin briefcase on to my lap. 'Let us say another thousand on account of special services today.'

He was squeezing again, but I didn't argue. He smilingly took his blood money with a hand that reminded me of a parrot's claw — a slow snatch.

Inside the station Grimsby sat me under a chart showing pictures of all the breeds of dog. Right then I decided that I was going to treat myself to one as soon as I could — a good rat-catcher probably, just to remind me of the lawyer who was at the moment scratching on one of the dreary doors.

Detective Inspector Probend made a point of ignoring Grimsby as he came out.

'Ah! Mr. Cox! Will you come in please?'

He went through all the motions of thanking me for calling and what have you.

Now Probend was usually pretty curt and to the point once the door was closed. This time, though, I noticed that his attitude was deferential. Not all that surprising really. After all, this job was a *big* one, and if he could cop me it would

74

excuse all of the other near misses. I gave him all of my attention.

'I'd like you to give me an account of your movements during the past twelve hours, Jack.'

Calling me Jack, that's what did it! Grimsby was always saying: 'Never trust a chummy policeman.' I decided to use each word as if it was a year of my life.

'I took my girl out until about eleven o'clock, and then spent the night at her flat.'

'And her name is?'

'Nelda,' I said. 'Nelda Thompson.'

'Where does she live?'

I gave him an address in Hampstead, but I was thinking of an underground safe vault – just a few miles away.

'Did you leave the place at all – say, around midnight?'

He had the time – right smack on the button. At eleven o'clock I screwed the brace to the floor. At half past the quarter-inch diamond drill was lined up with the centre of the dial and biting at a steady hundred turns a minute. Dead on the stroke of midnight I was blowing six ounces of cartridge powder down into the lock. But the Inspector wasn't supposed to be told that. 'No,' I said. 'I didn't leave her until after breakfast.'

'How long have you known Miss Thompson?'

'Years,' I answered.

At least, it seemed like years. Grimsby dug her up from somewhere and told me to be seen with her every night for a couple of weeks, just in case any awkward questions were asked around the neighbourhood. I even slept on her rotten kitchen chair a few times, just to add colour to the affair. But she was too much like Grimsby for my liking. Her handbag was stuffed with cash and all she could talk about was getting extra danger money. The only danger that she had to worry about was that somebody might tap her on the head for her roll of notes. I only hoped that my opinion of her didn't show on my face for Probend to see.

'Well, let's put it a different way, Jack,' he said. 'How well have you gotten along together?'

'Well enough to be able to have a shouting match sometimes,' I said. 'Almost as though we were married. In fact, we had one last night – I'm sure we must have woken up the neighbours.' I was on safe ground saying this, as Grimsby instructed Nelda to find a man and kick up a row about midnight.

Give Probend his due, he *does* have a sense of humour. My last remark had him smiling all over his face. 'All right, Jack,' he said, 'if that is your story, I'll just get it typed up and bring it back for your signature in a few minutes.'

As he went out of the door, Grimsby walked in.

'That Probend seems very pleased,' I said.

He spoke in a whisper. 'Can I be certain that you left no evidence – none at all?'

'Count on it,' I said. 'I didn't leave so much as a hair behind. And I wore a nylon over my face just in case there were any healthy old ladies taking notice.'

'In that case,' he said, 'we shall say that I telephoned you at the girl's flat at midnight, and I called there in person early this morning. I shall write my statement while we are waiting for the Inspector.'

I wondered how much extra *that* was going to cost me. 'How dependable is this so-called sweetheart of mine?'

'Now don't worry about that, Mr. Cox. Miss Thompson has a high regard for hard cash. If she were threatened for her money or her life, I rather think she would be hard put to make the choice.'

Which all sounded very comforting, but not enough to put me completely at ease.

I was glad to see Probend come back with the statement in his hand. Another few minutes and I could get the hell out of this place. And I would eat *alone*.

Probend carefully spread the papers in front of me. 'Now, I must ask you again before you sign this, Jack. Are you quite sure that you want to say that you spent all night with Miss Thompson?'

'Absolutely!'

What a thing to ask! I signed my name with a flourish.

Grimsby gave Probend his own statement. 'I can vouch for that, Inspector – as you will read from this.'

Probend folded our papers lovingly. 'Jack Cox – I hereby charge you with the murder of one, Nelda Thompson. Anything you say ... in fact, anything either of you say, may be given in evidence against you.'

Grimsby stood up. 'We have, for the moment,' he said, 'nothing further to say.'

Reprinted by permission of Fact & Fiction Agency

Chapter Thirteen

STORY IDEAS

By now, you will probably have started to itch at starting a short story of your own, and we encourage you to just finish reading the few more pages of this book – and then make an early start.

It is a curious fact that when ever the urge to write rises, there is often a completely blank mind on what to write about. The feeling is similar to having the strong desire to buy something for ourselves and finding that there is not overly much in the bank account.

What *not* to write about can soon be stated. Never write about anything of which you do not have at least some understanding and experience in order to give the story a ring of truth. If you wish to write that kind of story, then study the subject first. Next, from a purely professional point of view, never bother to write a story for which there is little or no market. Understand what markets exist before you even start. We must qualify this by saying that if you only wish to write for your own pleasure, then go ahead by writing on anything under the sun. But, if you aim to sell your work, you must certainly know that there will be a market for it. The painter may choose any subject and any technique, and, if the result is good, someone, somewhere, will surely buy the work at some time. The same cannot be said of the short story. It must be *aimed* at a market.

So, where do you get an idea for a story? If you have nothing tucked away in your head or in a notebook, then you must go hunting for the idea. We have already mentioned Georges Polti's thirty-six situations. We can also make another suggestion. Many story ideas may be derived from well-known and well-used proverbs. After all, if they are so well-known and well-used, they must have stood the test of time. We must believe that they contain the essence of truth, observation or wisdom or they would never have survived in common useage.

So that you will have no excuse for starting a short story fairly soon, let us give you a list of proverbs which you can refer to.

1. A bad penny always comes back.
2. A bad workman quarrels with his tools.
3. A beggar can never be bankrupt.
4. A blind man cannot judge colours.
5. A bow long bent grows weak.
6. A bully is always a coward.
7. A child may have too much of its mother's blessing.
8. A drowning man will clutch at a straw.
9. A dwarf on a giant's shoulders sees further of the two.
10. A fair exchange is no robbery.
11. A fool and his money are soon parted.
12. A fool may give a wise man counsel.
13. A forced kindness deserves no thanks.
14. A|fox is not taken twice in the same snare.
15. A friend is never known until needed.
16. A friend to all is a friend to none.
17. A great fortune is a great slavery.
18. A guilty conscience needs no accuser.
19. A lawyer never goes to law himself.
20. A liar is not believed when he speaks the truth.
21. A lie begets a lie.
22. A lion may be beholden to a mouse.
23. A lion's skin is never cheap.
24. A little body often harbours a good soul.
25. A maid that laughs is half taken.
26. A man can do no more than he can.
27. A man is known by the company he keeps.
28. A man surprised is half beaten.
29. A man without a smiling face must not open a shop.
30. A miss is as good as a mile.
31. A new broom sweeps clean.
32. A nod from a lord is a breakfast for a fool.
33. A nod is as good as a wink to a blind horse.
34. A pennyweight of love is worth a pound of law.
35. A pound of care will not pay an ounce of debt.
36. A rolling stone gathers no moss.
37. A runaway monk never praises his convent.
38. A saint abroad and a devil at home.

39. A small leak will sink a great ship.
40. A stick is quickly found to beat a dog with.
41. A stitch in time saves nine.
42. A thief knows a thief as a wolf knows a wolf.
43. A true jest is no jest.
44. A wise man changes his mind, a fool never will.
45. A woman conceals what she knows not.
46. A woman's advice is a poor thing, but he is a fool who does not take it.
47. A word spoken is past recalling.
48. A work ill done must be done twice.
49. Actions speak louder than words.
50. All are good lasses, but whence come the bad wives?

This is a start for your store of proverbs. You should add any more that come your way and have some kind of appeal to you.

Should you be interested, the germ of the idea which eventually became NOTHING TO SAY was mainly derived from Proverb 19 of this list – a lawyer never goes to law himself. The actual story has moved a long way from the proverb, but that is what was used as a starting-off point in looking for a story. Similarly, Proverb 22 – a lion may be beholden to a mouse, came into the idea which eventually became THE CON.

You should get into the habit of holding little thinking sessions with yourself in order to find story ideas. The more you do it, the easier it becomes. You have to remember a more modern American proverb – always quit when you are winning. As soon as you come up with one promising story idea in your thinking session, give thanks to whatever you bow to and call it a day.

Purely as an observation by the writer of this book, and certainly not as a natural law, it has always happened that taking a real live incident that actually happened and trying to dress it as fiction has never really been successful. It seems that the best fiction ideas have been just that – pure fiction.

Chapter Fourteen

YOU DON'T HAVE TO GET IT RIGHT FIRST TIME

'Not that the story need be long, but it will take a long while to make it short.' THOREAU

The story of writing the short story indeed may not be long, but it *has* taken some time for the telling. We have taken a close look at what is involved in successful writing, as far as the short story is concerned. And we have examined some published and one broadcast piece of work so that we can understand how certain techniques may be applied.

We should not pretend that the writing of fiction simply depends on learning a few slick tricks. Artistic talent, imagination and understanding one's fellow human beings also play important roles.

Author integrity and adding something worth while to one's culture may be added, without becoming a stuffy bore – although it would sometimes seem, these days, that one is on an uphill climb.

The main target for the author is the creating of believable characters who are well orchestrated in their relationship with each other and the line that the story follows. Given enough length, these characters are 'coloured' by the sets within which they operate, and they act out the story for the reader so that he *sees* what is going on and rarely hears the author's voice. The story should have some *purpose*, some seeming *significance*, and not be something which starts no-place and waffles along to a dreary end. The beginning should capture the interest of the reader, always providing it is the kind of story in which he or she is capable of showing an interest. We know that it is quite valid to look to authors of the past for both interest and example, but we always remember that writing fashions change and that we are writing for readers who live in today's world.

There is one further piece of advice which many writers could well paint on the wall over their typewriters:

YOU DON'T HAVE TO GET IT RIGHT FIRST TIME.

If you have any good sense you will never, ever show your first attempts at a story to anyone. Cut and change and polish until you *know* it is good. *Then* let it out of your hands. Many writers never fully appreciate the vast amount of freedom that they have to alter their work. They seem to think that their first stumbling draft of a story is engraved for all eternity and not a single line may be changed. What strange ideas we human beings get!

Get it down on paper however it comes out of your head, and then use whatever techniques you have learned to perfect it. You may be far more skilled at criticising other people's work than you are as a writer. In which case, you convince yourself that *you* never wrote anything as awful as this first draft — and then proceed to chop it to pieces and give plenty of gratuitous advice to the author. He is sure to thank you for it.

We cannot close without wheeling out one more proverb for you to consider:

It is better to read one poem a hundred times and keep it in your heart, than to read a hundred poems and remember them not at all.

Perhaps you may feel like browsing back through this book some time and check if there is anything else you could use to help you write your short stories!

END

Index